SONG OF THE NORTH

Books *by*

CLAIRE LEE PURDY

SONG OF THE NORTH
The Story of Edvard Grieg

HE HEARD AMERICA SING
The Story of Stephen Foster

Co-author of
MY BROTHER WAS MOZART

SONG of the NORTH

THE STORY OF EDVARD GRIEG

CLAIRE LEE PURDY

ILLUSTRATED BY

SUSANNE SUBA

JULIAN MESSNER INC.

PUBLISHED BY JULIAN MESSNER, INC.
8 WEST 40TH STREET, NEW YORK

PRINTED IN THE UNITED STATES OF AMERICA
BY MONTAUK BOOKBINDING CORPORATION, NEW YORK

FOR

ADOLPH S.

WHO PLAYS GRIEG'S MUSIC SO BEAUTIFULLY

ON HIS CONCERT ZITHER, AND WHO

WAS SO GENEROUS WITH

HIS HELP

ACKNOWLEDGMENTS

EXCERPTS from Edvard Grieg's correspondence and diary, from contemporary newspaper articles, and from the composer's autobiographical essay, "My First Success," are included in this book by courtesy of the American-Scandinavian Foundation, from whose publication *Edvard Grieg,* by David Monrad-Johansen, translated by Madge Robertson (Princeton University Press), the quotations were taken. The author of the present book wishes to thank Miss Hanna Astrup Larsen, Literary Secretary of the American-Scandinavian Foundation and editor of its magazine, the *Review,* and all other members of the Foundation, for their gracious co-operation.

Quotations from the correspondence of Johannes Brahms and Elisabet and Heinrich Herzogenberg are included by permission of E. P. Dutton and Company from their publication *Johannes Brahms: The Herzogenberg Correspondence* (1909), edited by Max Kalbeck, translated into English by Hannah Bryant.

Excerpts from Tchaikovsky's correspondence and diary are taken from *The Life and Letters of Peter Ilich Tchaikovsky,* by Modeste Tchaikovsky, edited by Rosa Newmarch, by permission of Dodd, Mead & Company, New York, United States and Canadian agents for Peters Edition, Leipzig.

All music from the original C. F. Peters, Leipzig, editions is included by special arrangement with the Peters representative in the United States: The Clayton F. Summy Co., Chicago and New York.

Arrangements of Grieg's music borrowed from collections and critical works are included by permission of the publishers of these works, listed as follows:

Excerpts from Op. 27 and Op. 36: *Chamber Music,* by Thomas F. Dunhill. By permission of the Macmillan Company, New York.

Excerpts from Op. 1, No. 1; Op. 3, No. 3; Op. 68, No. 4; Op. 73, No. 7: *Piano Lyrics and Shorter Compositions of Edvard Grieg,* edited by Bertha Feiring Tapper. Excerpts from Op. 23, No. 1: *Fifty Songs by Edvard Grieg,* edited by Henry T. Finck. Excerpts from Op. 16 and Op. 24: *Larger Piano Compositions of Edvard Grieg,* edited by Bertha Feiring Tapper. By permission of Oliver Ditson Company, Boston: Theodore Presser Co., Philadelphia, agents.

Excerpt from Op. 55, No. 1: *Schirmer's Library,* Volume 1420 (contains complete work). Excerpt from Op. 68, No. 1: Grieg Album of the *Master Series for the Young* (contains complete work). By permission of G. Schirmer, Inc., New York.

Her publisher joins her also in thanks to Elizabeth C. Moore for the editorial supervision of the book and the verification of its material.

Claire Lee Purdy
Julian Messner, Inc.

NOTE TO THE READER

In the back of the book will be found a complete list of Grieg's works, arranged in the order of their opus numbers; examples of his music as mentioned in the text; a bibliography; and two indexes.

SONG OF THE NORTH

Chapter One

*. . . creeping like snail
Unwillingly to school.*
AS YOU LIKE IT

THE sun had been shining since early morning. That is why all the sensible folk of Bergen were hurrying about the streets in the early forenoon with umbrellas, raincoats, rubbers, and galoshes. They knew that a town with five feet of rainfall every year had reached its limit of sunshine for one spring day. The rain would soon be pelting down.

One citizen of Bergen, however, walked slowly along, with now and then a look of anxious inquiry at the sky, as if he feared that rain would not fall on Bergen's roof-tops that day. This citizen was very young—not quite eight years old, in fact.

"I hope it's going to rain, going to rain, going to rain," he chanted.

Soft, straight hair, pale as northern sunlight, touched the shoulders of his schoolboy's blouse. Eyes blue-gray, like the Norwegian fjords with the mists upon them, and a gleam of the Old Nick in their depths, gazed with candid pleasure at the clouds piling up seaward.

As the boy's sturdy boots clomped along the narrow stone-paved way called the Strandgaten, a salt breeze from the North Sea sent the clouds scudding under the sun. Laughing and frisking about, the youngster held out his hands to catch the first heavy drops. He turned his snub nose up to the gray sky and made chuckling noises such as the old grandmothers of Norway said were made only by the water nixies and the "little folk" who lived under Bergen's seven hills.

It was not long before the warm rain had made the boy's clothing smell like a flock of sheep on a rain-soaked mountainside. His fair hair hung down in flat strands, and bright drops dripped from it into his collar. Presently, the clouds went skimming on their way before the westerly wind, and the sun came out to make the streets and houses steam. The boy stopped his capering, felt the sleeve of his blouse, and frowned.

"Not wet enough," he muttered.

Looking about him in a way that told that matters of this sort were familiar to him, he discovered a spout through which the gutter along the roof of a little bakery was emptying its rainwater. Chirruping like an imp, he skipped over to the spout and stood under the pouring water until he was quite as wet as a seine drawn up from the sea.

"Edvard Grieg!"

The boy jumped in his skin at the name, but did not turn his head toward the old gentleman in rain-cape and galoshes who was walking toward him. There was no need to look, for Edvard knew by the commanding sound of the deep voice that the old Stiftamtmann (Provincial Governor), his grandfather, had discovered the strange antics under the spout.

"In the name of all the trolls in Norway, and of the three billy goats gruff besides, why are you dallying along the street when you should have been at your school desk an hour ago? And what are you doing under that spout, Edvard?" the old man bellowed. "Or *is* this Edvard?" Taking one of the boy's ears none too gently between strong thumb and forefinger, he forced his grandson to look at him. "*Are* you Edvard Grieg, son of Alexander Grieg, respected merchant of Bergen, or some drenched, homeless puppy? Or maybe you are one of the little people from the hills, a troll child, and not our Edvard at all! All right, young man, explain! What were you doing under that spout?"

"Getting wet, Grandfather Hagerup," said Edvard meekly.

"And impudent, too! Getting wet! Don't you think I can see that, young man? But why were you getting wet?"

"So that I shouldn't have to go to school today. Whenever I get wet like this the schoolmaster sends me home at once. And Mother sometimes keeps me home next day, too. She's afraid of lung sickness."

"You don't say so!" The tall old gentleman brought his white brows together in a ferocious frown, though truth to tell, he did so more to hide the amusement in his own eyes than to frighten his grandson. "That explains your schoolmaster's remarks to me some weeks ago. 'Why is it,' he asked, 'that Edvard and his brother can set out for school together in the rain, both with overcoats and rain-capes; yet Edvard invariably arrives so wet that he must be sent home, whereas his brother John is only moderately damp?' And by the way, where is John this morning?" the old man asked, removing his own warm cape to wrap it around the shivering boy.

"He went on ahead," explained Edvard, hanging his head and speaking in a very small voice. "He said he didn't see how all the trouble I gave myself was worth the reward of staying out of school. He said I would just have to make up the lessons I missed, and the schoolmaster would be twice as stern, and that the ugly old schoolhouse wouldn't turn into a fairy grotto no matter how long I stayed away."

"And he was quite right, too. John is a good, sensible fellow, and he doesn't let his Norwegian imagination run away with him the way you do, Edvard. You should try to be more like your elder brother, boy."

"Yes, Grandfather, I do try, but sometimes I think it's a lost cause."

"Lost cause, indeed!" The Stiftamtmann struggled to hide his amusement. "There'll be an end of this nonsense when I tell your mother."

"I rather hoped you wouldn't tell her." Edvard spoke in a subdued way.

"Oh? And what made you imagine that I would suppress such news?"

"Well, you see, Mother is very busy, what with looking after Maren and Ingeborg and Elisabeth and John—"

"And you, my fine young water eel! You give your mother more cause for worry than all the rest of the children, I'll wager."

"I'm afraid so," agreed Edvard. "And there are the baking and scrubbing and laundering to oversee." He went on explaining his mother's duties. "And her concerts and my piano lessons. I'm afraid I give her trouble with the lessons, too. You see, she's frightfully particular about my striking the right note."

"Hum. I'll be bound she is. Hum. Yes. And what if I *do* agree to keep word of your disgraceful conduct from her?"

"I shall improve in my school work. I shall study history and maps and dry grammar—even though my back breaks!"

The Stiftamtmann threw back his shaggy old head and laughed until several passers-by glanced curiously at the old man and the boy muffled in the big cape. "Now you sound like your mother! How often have I heard her say, 'Energy is the main thing. I shall work though my back breaks.' "

"Yes," sighed Edvard. "Mother is much fonder of hard work than I am."

"Well, come along, you young kobold. I'll go home with you. And I'll keep this waterspout business to myself, in view of the promises you have made."

Edvard was all smiles again. "I knew you would," he crowed. "You are really a very satisfactory grandfather. But where are you going after you take me home? To the fishmarket?"

"The fishmarket is right."

"May I go with you?" Edvard was all excitement.

"Upon my soul, Edvard, I believe you'd rather smell fish at the market of the Triangle than the flowers of Asgard! No, you may not come with me today. But perhaps tomorrow, after school, I'll come by for you," Grandfather Hagerup added, and Edvard had to be content.

"Where is Asgard?" Edvard wanted to know after a short, thoughtful silence.

"Asgard isn't a real place," explained his grandfather. "Of course, our Viking ancestors believed it was. They were pagans, you know—believed in all sorts of gods like Odin and Balder and Thor. The place where these gods were supposed to live was called Asgard."

"Where did they think it was?"

"At the very center of the universe. And the only way to Asgard was over the rainbow-bridge called *Bifrost*."

"Look! There is Bifrost now!" Edvard was pointing excitedly at a red and purple rainbow made by the meeting of sun's rays and raindrops over the mist-covered mountains behind the city.

"Just as the old Vikings saw it, probably," agreed his

grandfather. "Over that bridge only the gods and those favored by the gods could ride, and on the other side were many regions and mansions, including *Valhalla.*"

"What was Valhalla like?" prompted Edvard. It was a rare thing to find Grandfather in a mood to tell the old tales of Viking land, and Edvard wanted to make the most of the old man's fanciful flight.

"Valhalla? Oh, it was a great hall, like the mead halls built by all rich Vikings and Viking rulers. Spears were its rafters, and shields its roof. Odin the one-eyed, greatest of all gods, ruler of the winds, sat there on his raised throne at the end of the long table, and his wolves were beside him. At the table itself sat the warriors of earth who had died heroically in battle, brought to this hall of Asgard by the fateful women known as the *Valkyries.* Odin and the warriors were wont to drink mead together from great horns or the skulls of vanquished warriors. They would fall to quarreling, and then there was fighting till each warrior was slain again. But each morning the slain were wakened to life by the crowing of the cock called Golden-Comb. And round the great hall the river Thund flowed, and in it swam the sun."

"Did all the Viking warriors go to Valhalla?"

"Oh, no. Only those especially chosen by the Valkyries. Others slain in battle went to Freya's hall in Vanir, to the dwelling called Folk-Plain. Freya was both goddess of love and the 'possessor of the slain'."

"But suppose a Viking didn't die in battle?"

"Then, my boy, he joined the rest of the ordinary folks and went down the troublesome *Helveg* to the abode of the dead called *Hel.* There the Queen of the Dead, daughter of the god Loki, dwelt beneath the roots of the sacred ash *Yggdrasil,* where she waited for the day when the great tree should quake and the *Twilight of the gods* (the end of earth and heaven, too) should come. And though the end of all creation did not come, the doom of the gods arrived, in a manner of speaking; for all the old gods disappeared from the land after Olaf Trygvason and St. Olaf, who came after, brought a new faith to Norway—the Christian faith."

"Tell me about Olaf Trygvason and St. Olaf," begged Edvard, but the old Stiftamtmann merely pointed to the doorway before them. They were on Edvard's own doorstep. Beyond the heavy oak door with its polished brass knocker someone was playing the piano.

"Listen, Edvard. Your mother is playing. Something by Mozart, isn't it?"

"Yes, it's Mozart's Sonata in G major." Edvard identified the music without hesitation, and was all unconscious of the look, half of surprise and half of admiration, which his grandfather gave him. The old man said nothing of the pride he felt in his grandson's musical knowledge, however, for it is foreign to the reserved Norwegian nature to spend breath in compliments. A look or a smile is praise enough.

A brisk rapping brought the Griegs' maidservant, Ingrid, to the door. She was a rosy-cheeked peasant girl, in the short full skirt and colorful bodice of the Valdres region, which had been her home before she came to take service in Bergen.

"Mercy on us!" exclaimed the girl. "Are you home wet to the skin again, Edvard Grieg?"

Edvard's grandfather cautioned the girl to quiet. "We needn't disturb his mother, need we?"

"Of course not, Herr Hagerup. Nurse and I will attend to the young rascal."

"Thank you, Ingrid. Tell my daughter I could not stop today." Grandfather shook a warning finger at Edvard. "Remember your promise! No water spouts tomorrow!"

"No spout *tomorrow*," agreed Edvard, grinning because he had not had to make any promises about the day after tomorrow or the day after that.

Grandfather Hagerup took his rain-cape from the boy's shoulders and prepared to go on his way. Ingrid saw him to the door and returned scolding to Edvard.

"I'll turn you over to Nurse, that's what I'll do. She'll warm you, I'll warrant, where it will do the most good. Missing school, the way you do!" Ingrid hustled Edvard past the door of the drawing-room, where his mother was playing, into the big square kitchen.

A tall, elderly woman wearing the spotless white Bergen cap with its flaring sides and wimple-like fitting turned as Edvard entered the kitchen with the maid.

"Some dry clothes, Nurse, for the young master," explained Ingrid briefly before she left to go about her duties of sweeping and dusting.

"Dry clothes again, eh? I have a notion to turn you across my lap, as I did when you were a small boy, and give you one or two stinging smacks just for luck," declared the old nurse. "Well, here are some dry clothes, warm from pressing. And some dry boots, too, freshly shined, more's the pity," she grumbled.

Turning her back to Edvard, the tall woman took up her ironing again. Edvard was left to pull and haul at his wet clothes as best he could. "And what are you planning to do now?" Nurse inquired.

"I don't know exactly. I wanted to go with Grandfather to the fishmarket, but he wouldn't let me," explained Edvard.

"Huh. That's no surprise. Some day you're going to turn into a salmon, the way Loki did, and the fishmongers will be selling you at the stalls, along with their poor jokes to keep the customer's mind from dwelling too much on the price they're charging."

"I know about Loki," said Edvard proudly. "Grandfather just told me. Loki was the father of the Queen of the Dead, who lived under the roots of the ash tree Yggdrasil."

"He was more than that." The tall woman tested one of the heavy irons heating on the cookstove, shook her head, and put the iron back to heat some more. "Loki," she explained, "was the god of strife, the very spirit of evil. It was Loki who brought about the death of Balder, god of light, by arming blind Hodhr with a weapon of mistletoe, the only thing capable of harming Balder. He was a sly one, that Loki, with his fair face and his black heart."

"But how did he get turned into a salmon?" Edvard was busy pulling a dry woolen blouse over his head.

"Oh, he did that himself, in order to escape Odin's

anger after Balder was killed. In the form of a salmon Loki hid under a waterfall, thinking that no one would search for him in such a place. But the gods soon discovered his hiding place, and with a net Thor, god of war and thunder, waded into midstream. Loki tried to leap over the net. Thor caught him in his hands. Loki managed to wriggle through Thor's hands, but Thor grasped his tail so firmly that it was tapering when Loki at last got free. And that's why the tails of salmon are tapering to this very day."

The nurse became aware of the sound of grunting and struggling behind her. "What in the world are you making such a fuss about?" She turned to stare at Edvard, who was making a comical face as he pulled frantically at his boots.

"My stockings are too thick," complained Edvard. "I can't pull my boots on over such horse blankets!"

"Nonsense. Those are the good wool socks your mother knitted for you. Put *can't* away from you, boy, and take hold with both hands. That's the only way to succeed in anything."

Hands on hips, she stood over the struggling and red-faced Edvard until, unassisted, he had pulled the boots on.

"There, you see? You don't need your old nurse any more for tasks like that."

When Edvard was warm and dry once more, he settled himself contentedly in a chair by the stove. Nurse finished her ironing and began to lay out material for cookie baking.

"Tell me a story, will you, Nurse?"

At that moment, Baby Elisabeth, a little girl of six, discovered that her beloved Edvard was home. She came running down the stairs from the playroom, and climbed immediately into her brother's lap. Nurse smiled to see the two blond heads snuggled together.

"Please tell a story." Elisabeth added her voice to that of her brother. Whatever Edvard wanted was good enough for the little sister.

"Oh, you two and your stories! You must think I am a book of fairy tales, I declare! What can I tell you that you haven't heard ten times over?"

"It doesn't matter. Tell us about the husband that was left at home to mind the house," suggested Edvard, and Elisabeth nodded her head vigorously.

"Well, once upon a time, there was a farmer and his wife. The wife was always grumbling that she had too much work to do. 'While you are out in the fields with nothing to do but plow, I must bake, and tend the fire, see that our cow is fed and milked, look after the baby, clean the house, and do the washing. I think it's most unfair.'

"Finally the farmer got tired of all this complaining. He said to his wife, 'You are making a whole glacier out of the ice on the waterbucket. I'll show you how easy your tasks are. We'll make a bargain. Tomorrow, you take the horses and plow to the field and I'll stay home to mind the house.'"

At this point Edvard and Elisabeth giggled. They both knew well what was to follow.

"So they agreed to do each other's work," Nurse went

on. "The wife started out early for the field, and the husband stayed at home."

" 'What nonsense my wife has been talking!' he said to himself. 'Why, there isn't enough work here to keep me busy. Now let me see, what shall I do first?'

"He decided to add fuel to the fire and set a pot of mush to cooking. While he was gone for the wood, the baby woke up and was crying lustily when he returned. He rocked the cradle until the baby was asleep again, and then he went out to the well to get some water. While he was gone, the old cow broke her rope and was wandering in the pasture, close to the edge of the deep fjord, when he caught her. While he was leading her back to the house, he stumbled over a big rock and bruised himself pretty badly.

"When the cow was tied up again, the husband ran back to put the mush on the fire. But the fire had burned itself out while he was catching the cow. It took him a long while to rebuild it, for the baby kept waking up and had to be rocked. Just as he set the pot of water on the blaze, the baby woke up and the old cow began to bawl. The husband carried the baby out with him while he milked the cow, and he had a pretty hard time of it, what with the cow kicking over the pail whenever he had to run back to the house to stir the porridge. He had but a bare cupful of milk when he was done, and the fire was burning low again. He took the baby back to the house while he added fuel to the embers. Then the old cow broke her rope again.

" 'I'll fix you!' cried the exasperated husband. So he hauled the cow up to the low thatch roof of the cottage. The free end of her rope he threw down the chimney, and, running into the house, he tied the rope to his leg. At that moment the terrified cow slipped from the roof, and into the fireplace went the yelling husband. And there his good wife found him, kicking and sputtering, with his head in the porridge. That was how the husband fared who stayed at home to mind the house," Nurse wound up her story.

"Snip, snap, snout!

"This tale's told out!"

she cried so suddenly that Edvard and Elisabeth jumped in surprise. The three were laughing merrily when Mother Grieg came in.

"Edvard, Edvard! Home again on a school day?" She shook her head in stern reproval. "Well, since you're here, you can improve your time by learning your piano lesson. I'll help with *middag*," she added to Nurse as she tied an apron of generous proportions around her waist. "Energy is the main thing. Remember that, Edvard!"

Chapter Two

· And thereby hangs a tale.'
AS YOU LIKE IT

AFTER a lecture from his parents, Edvard went dutifully to school next day. He hardly minded the scolding he received from the stern schoolmaster; for all day he was thinking to himself, "Grandfather is going to call for me after school today."

True to his promise the old Stiftamtmann was waiting when Edvard arrived home. Nurse provided her young charge with an extra sweater, for the spring afternoons were still cold.

"Now off with you," she said. "And mind you tell me everything you see and hear. See all the sights and listen quietly to the talk of others. Sharp eyes and a still tongue make a man wise. That is advice to remember, Edvard."

"I'll remember," promised Edvard.

17

"Come then," cried Grandfather gaily. "We'll be off the Tyskebrygge and the Old German Wharf—and the Triangle, too, if our legs hold out."

They took the first turning, which led them out of Strandgaten, and followed many a winding way where the gable ends of the houses leaned across to each other just as some of these same houses had done almost two hundred years before, in the time of the great poet-philosopher Holberg. When Edvard and his grandfather came to the waterfront street called Tyskebrygge, a spanking breeze was blowing across the harbor.

All manner of craft moved in the choppy water: row-boats and flat barges, coastwise passenger boats, fishing smacks, and a few old-time Norwegian *jagts* with high prows and square sails that revealed their descent from the dragon-ships of Viking days. Big boats and little were tied up at the old wharf. Fishing nets were spread out to dry, and here and there a group of old sailors, still jaunty in their salty blue jackets, white hair showing under the round seamen's caps, swapped yarns and rolled biting Copenhagen snuff under their tongues.

Edvard, mindful of his old nurse's advice, kept his blue eyes open and said hardly a word as he walked along the quay. This was the old German Quay, where the merchants of the Hanseatic League had done business with the Norwegians from the year 1350 to 1700. Some of the dark old buildings, the *gaards* or warehouses, still stood.

Holding Edvard up to one of the narrow windows so that he could see the ancient desk and high stools, Grandfather Hagerup told about the old scales used by the merchants of the Hansa. Two sets were always in use—one set made to "weigh short" in selling, the other to "weigh heavy" for buying purposes.

Edvard heard how the penniless German clerks were held virtual prisoners in these old *gaards,* held to their tasks by the exacting merchants and their managers, not allowed to mingle socially with the townspeople. He learned about the strange monopoly of trade which the Hansa merchants enforced with the sword.

"Oh, how those 'Knights of the Fleecing' did cheat the Norwegians! And with what lordly contempt did they view their poor dupes! But like all tyrants, they over-reached themselves. The Norwegians finally rose in fury and drove the Hansa merchants from the land forever. Before that happy day arrived, however, the German wolves were much harassed by a certain Norwegian gentleman called 'Little Sir Alf' Erlingsson."

"Please tell me about him," begged Edvard. "Was he a pirate?"

"Well, he was called that, yes. But I should say he was more like a Robin Hood. We know little of actual fact about him, but many legends of his impudence and daring have come down to us. He was a mysterious little figure, a Norwegian baron who dedicated his life to hounding the German merchants. He lived on a faraway fjord, where he had a large farm, many good boats, and not a few loyal friends and neighbors. He and these daredevil friends sallied forth in every kind of weather, much as their Viking ancestors had done in the long journeys to every port of Christendom; but Sir Alf's purpose was to harry and vex only the merchants of the Hansa.

"Sir Alf and his men would lay all sorts of traps for the German merchants. Once, several of the 'gentlemen pirates' sailed boldly into the harbor of Bergen and told of a huge catch of cod not ten leagues to the north. So many cod had been caught, they declared, that fifty boats as large as their own would not carry them. This miraculous catch was being salted and dried and would be for sale for a mere song if the Hansa merchants would bring ships to carry off the tons of fish.

"The greedy merchants rose to the bait and sent three of their best ships to bring in the cod. They were lured into a desolate inlet by the men who had told of the catch, and there they were set upon by Sir Alf and his men. The Hansa boats were captured, and their captains and crews considered themselves lucky that they found their way back to Bergen on crude rafts. The trees for these rafts were cut with the axes left to the Hansa sailors by Sir Alf with mocking chivalry.

"Little Sir Alf led the hated merchants on many another such wild-goose chase. Expedition after expedition sent out to capture him resulted in whole ships' crews being captured and held for ransom. How the Hansa merchants fumed and ranted when they had to hand over some of their money bags to save the skins of their fellow merchants!

"Sir Alf's most daring trick was to come disguised right up to the German Quay. There he bargained long and shrewdly, telling the merchants that he could reveal the exact location of Sir Alf's hiding place if he were paid his price. He received his gold and drew an elaborate map. It was so elaborate, in fact, that it led the Hansa ships in circles, far away from where Sir Alf was by that time, you may be sure."

The Stiftamtmann had business to attend to at one of the warehouses on the quay. With a word of warning about keeping out of the way of dray horses and loads of cargo swinging from ships' booms, he left Edvard to wander alone for a while along the busy wharf. Edvard, unnoticed by the people of the waterfront, missed no detail of their work or fun.

Fish carts were loading fish and lobsters from the small boats, with cart owners and fishermen keeping up a running fire of conversation as to the state of the weather, the size of the fish runs, the probability of a large catch by the Lofoten Island men that year, and many more matters vital to their business. Large drays pulled by powerful horses rumbled up and down between warehouse and warehouse, loading and unloading bales of hides, furs, boxes of woolen goods, and fragrant boards of pine and fir. Sailors from foreign ports, on leave between unloading time and sailing time, walked arm in arm, seeing the sights of Bergen's dock. They called out, as sailors will, in English or Italian or Spanish to an occasional peasant girl dressed in the colorful costume of her native valley or fjord, hurrying demurely past on her way to the fish-market to do some last-minute shopping for her employer. Food peddlers cried their wares—crisp fried fish, shrimps, potatoes, and good Norwegian bread and sweet rolls.

The stevedores sang as they swung gigantic loads to

the booms of the freight vessels. Their songs were mostly the strange minor tunes of Norway's lonely valleys and deep, winding fjords, those strange arms of the sea which extend far into the land. These songs were as beautifully wild as the old Viking, Olaf Trygvason, sailing over the North Sea to Norway to destroy the old gods of his people; as tender as poor Jófrid's lullaby for her lost girl-child; sometimes as melancholy as the long winter twilights of Norway; again as robustly gay as the dances of the peasants around the bonfires on St. John's Eve. Edvard listened, absorbing the strange rhythms and quaint tone combinations without knowing that he did.

Grandfather Hagerup was gone a long while. When he rejoined Edvard, the sun, which was dropping toward the western sea, was being threatened by heavy rain clouds; and Edvard was beginning to eye the food stalls wistfully.

"Ho! Hungry, are you?" cried his grandfather. "Very well. We'll have our dinner at Nils' Place."

Nils' Place was a cozy little café, with scrubbed pine tables and a waitress with face so bright that she might have been scrubbed with the same sand that polished the tables. She made a joke with Grandfather and playfully ruffled Edvard's hair. Then she brought them their dinner —steaming fish soup with parsley floating on it, a little brown cheese, nippy and strong, and *fladbröd*, the Norwegian rye bread which is rolled out as thin as a wafer and round as a cartwheel. There was wine for Grandfather and milk for Edvard.

While they ate, Edvard's grandfather told more tales of the early days of Bergen's history. He told about Nor-

way's popular hero, King Sverre, who with a mere hand-
ful of ragged men called "birchlegs" took the proud city
of Bergen in the twelfth century. In the next century, the
great king of Norway was Haakon the Old. Grandfather
Hagerup told how Haakon had ordered built a great hall
to celebrate his coronation. This hall, as Edvard well
knew, still stood, near the Triangle, with its great mead
table and rude benches still in place and wild barbaric
drawings on its walls. Once the great hall had echoed to
the robust laughter of the last of the Vikings and to the
spirited declaiming of the skalds, the minstrels who
sang of the deeds of the illustrious dead. Now the old pile
stood forlorn and empty, and no fire ever burned on its
wide hearth any more.

"You didn't tell me about Olaf Trygvason and St.
Olaf." Edvard reminded his grandfather of their conversation the day before.

"Olaf Trygvason was the son of a Norwegian king.
As a child, Olaf was sent over the sea to England. There
he became a Christian. In the tenth century, he returned
to his native land. After many hard-fought battles, this
mightiest of Norway's sons was crowned king. Olaf Trygvason was a fierce, handsome man. The old sagas tell of
his blue eyes flashing fire like the ice of the glaciers and
his beard and long hair blowing in the wind as he stood
at the prow of his long ship. A mighty arm he had, and
none could stand up before him when he swung the
heavy battle-ax that most men could not even lift. His
voice was like thunder; yet he could make it tender and
sweet, too, to sing a love song, and he played the harp

like any skald, for this art he had learned from the Irish harpers.

"Yes, Olaf Trygvason was a wild, strange man. He was determined to make Christians of his people, if he had to kill most of them to do it! He made his capital at Trondhjem, where the stern northern winters and sparkling summers suited his own changeable moods. He and the half-mad warriors called *berserks,* who followed Olaf with fanatic devotion, would descend on some temple dedicated to the worship of Thor or Frey, destroy its idols, and kill all worshipers who would not then and there deny their old faith.

"Olaf Trygvason was killed fighting the Norsemen who refused to embrace Christianity. At his death, Olaf Haraldsson was crowned king—he was the Olaf who became St. Olaf. Like Trygvason, he forced the Christian faith on his people. A strange saint, you will think him, bringing the faith of the peaceful Christ to his people at the point of a Viking sword, but I suppose he did as he thought right. And those days were wild and cruel, my lad," Edvard's grandfather wound up his story. "And now if you've had enough romancing for one day, let's pay the good serving girl and be on our way."

Edvard was very quiet as they walked along the crowded waterfront streets. The rain was falling, soft and warm, and Edvard walked cautiously in the shelter of his grandfather's umbrella. Thinking over all that his grandfather had told him, he saw in imagination the old Vikings heaving at the long oars of their dragon-ships, with a Viking chieftain like Olaf Trygvason in white tunic and silver belt, fur-lined boots, short sword at waist, standing sentinel at the prow. On shore were the crude boat shelters where the proud dragon-ships spent the winters, waiting for spring to spread their gorgeous striped sails to the wind. In the great mead halls the Vikings likewise waited for the annual spring journey to foreign lands. While winter winds and rains made the outdoors bleak and cold they were snug enough, feasting and drinking.

With the men were the Viking women—sisters, wives and daughters—in short kirtle skirts and fur-lined robes. They were proud women, respected and independent as the women of a later day were no longer to be.

Shields and swords and spears were hung along the walls of the hall; horns of mead stood on the table; savory joints hissed and sputtered on spits over the roaring fire. In the warmest corner the minstrel with his harp sat singing his verses about the heroes who feasted with Odin in Valhalla.

Edvard's dreaming mood was shattered as soon as he and his grandfather neared the Triangle. Row upon row of stalls lined the open space left for the fishmarket between warehouses and shops. A strong smell of fish hung heavily in the rain-laden air. On every side were stalls with mackerel, herring, salmon, sea trout, a dozen kinds of shellfish, barrels of salt fish.

Stout women, with arms muscular from hauling at the seines and drawing the fishcarts along the quay, slapped fish upon the scales swinging beside the whale-oil lamps. The fishwives kept up an incessant chatter and shouting and laughing. Their talk was salty, full of expressions from seaport towns far to the north. Most of them spoke a folk language called the *Landsmaal*—the old Norse language which was not taught in the schools. The Danish-Norwegian tongue was the language of educated folk. The fish peddlers enlivened their speech with expressions in the dialects of various faraway valleys and mountain districts. Everyone seemed to be in a merry mood; and no one seemed to mind the rain.

"Look!" shouted an old fish woman. "A salmon as red as Loki, and nearly as sly; for may I never sell another fish if this monster did not come near to overleaping the gun'ls of the boat after he was caught!" The fish she held up for inspection was a salmon of less than usual size. Her customers caught the joke and laughed with her. Edvard was pleased that he knew what she meant when she compared the salmon to Loki.

Another fish merchant—this one a tall, old man with a drooping mustache as yellow as taffy—called out in a rasping voice:

"Fish! Fish! Fish!
Try our cod and herring;
They make a tasty dish."

His voice reminded Edvard of the coarse cry of the male sea lions that sometimes sunned themselves on rocky Norwegian beaches.

A fat little man who might have been a gnome, thought Edvard, called out slyly: "Come buy, come buy! I have the *only* fish in the market. There's none better and none worse, and that's a fact."

Grandfather made a purchase or two. Then he and Edvard turned their tired feet homeward. The pavements were glistening wet in the narrow streets which led them from the Triangle to Strandgaten. Miniature shops with quaint wooden signs hanging above their doors were aglow with light beyond windows streaming with rain.

"All this," said Edvard's grandfather, "is much the same as it was during Holberg's day. I often imagine I may meet some of the motley company of his great books at the next turning. Do you know who Holberg was, lad?"

"Well—" began Edvard uncertainly.

"I see you don't. What do they teach you youngsters in that dreary school? Holberg was born right here in Bergen," he went on. "That was long ago, in the seventeenth century. He went to Denmark in his youth and educated himself. He found that there were no books written in the native language of the people. The Danes scorned the Danish folk tongue, much as we do the Landsmaal of the fishmarket. It has been said that a wealthy Dane wrote his letters in Latin, spoke to his wife and his friends in French, called his dogs in German, spoke only to his servants in Danish. Well, Holberg changed all that. He began to write books—satires, comedies, books on law, politics, science, philosophy—all in the Danish tongue. He even wrote travel books to tell the Danes how his native Norway looked."

With his head stuffed with these many tales of Bergen's colorful past, Edvard came home tired and happy. Grandfather turned Edvard over to Nurse before he tiptoed into the drawing-room, where Edvard's mother and her friends were giving an amateur performance of Mozart's opera *The Marriage of Figaro.* Edvard snuggled down in his bed and listened with pleasure to the faint sounds of music wafted up the staircase. What the performers lacked in technique and voice they made up in appreciation of the great music they sang. Many an amateur performance in the Grieg drawing-room was more inspired than a professional opera performed to order in some cold auditorium.

Chapter Three

Then heigh-ho! the holly!
This life is most jolly.
AS YOU LIKE IT

𝓘T WAS Christmas Eve in the year 1852. Holly and evergreen and mistletoe hung at every window of the Grieg household, and soft candle-light made a cozy glow in every room. Edvard, a slender lad of nine years, was seated at the piano in his mother's drawing-room. He was pleasantly aware, as he ran his nimble fingers lightly over the keys, of mysterious rustlings and hushed laughter, quick footsteps and hasty whisperings throughout the house. The *Jul* preparations, which had been going on for weeks, were reaching a climax, with everyone at some last-minute task. Edvard's mother was strict about regular duties, however; that is why Edvard sat practicing at the usual hour, in spite of the exciting approach of the Yule season.

As Edvard played he was thinking of something other than Christmas, or the music before him. He was thinking, in fact, that now that he was almost a man he had better settle down and stop the nonsense of standing under water spouts to keep from going to school. A fellow could grow up as ignorant as a crow, if he weren't careful. Besides, Edvard had just made a momentous decision. He had decided on his life's work.

An inspired sermon by the Lutheran minister of the church which the Grieg family attended had settled Edvard's problem of choosing his profession. Nothing could be more satisfactory than making sermons, he had decided. He would be a minister, and it was a great relief to have the matter settled. He heaved a sigh of satisfaction and struck a loud chord with his two hands, then another and another, to express his complete approval of the world and everyone in it including nine-year-old Edvard Grieg.

"Edvard!" A stern voice called from the kitchen.

"Yes, Mother?" Edvard held down the keys which had sounded the last crashing chord.

"You are not practicing properly."

"I shall go back to the music right away," promised Edvard, obediently turning the pages of his exercise book to select a study built on the scale of G minor.

Striking the first chord with a will, Edvard plunged into the study with gusto. Deft fingering and careful attention to modulations were evidence of considerable skill and many hours of study on the part of the young performer. The fact was that Edvard had been studying music since he was six years old, with his talented mother for teacher and supervisor of practice hours.

As a young girl, Gesine Hagerup had been given the best instruction that money could obtain in Bergen. She showed such talent that her father—Edvard's Grandfather Hagerup—had allowed her to continue her education abroad, an unusual privilege for a girl in her day. She had gone to Hamburg to study piano and singing and the theory of music with the well-known conductor, Methfessel, and returned to play an important part in the musical life of Bergen.

Edvard was giving his entire attention to the study before him when his mother appeared silently in the doorway. She was a tall, handsome woman, with strong, characterful features. If there was something overstern about her mouth it may have been the result of a certain unhappy event of her youth. Gossip had it that Gesine Judith Hagerup had fallen in love with a young sailor, but that the match was forbidden by her father. The choice he made—young Alexander Grieg, son of the prosperous merchant John Grieg—was forced upon his daughter after the custom of those days. However that might have been, Gesine Judith was a good wife and a devoted mother, who provided a well-ordered, cheerful home for her family.

Edvard's old nurse joined his mother. "You may believe me or not," she whispered to her employer, "but that child has talent of an uncommon sort."

"I know," his mother whispered back. "I do not tell him so; for he is such a dreamer that he would think his talent a substitute for hard work, I fear. But I know. He will be great some day. God has been good to the boy." Edvard's mother was a devoutly religious woman, humble in her belief that all talent and genius was a divine gift, to be accepted with thanksgiving and not with arrogance.

Edvard, playing crashing chords and brilliant runs in G minor, heard not a word of this whispered conference. Presently his mother and Nurse stole back to the kitchen. Such preparations as were on foot in that kitchen! Ingrid, who came from the country and understood such matters, had made a bewildering variety of pork and veal sausages. She was busily slicing some of these, revealing the patterns of stars and spirals which she had managed by some Norwegian witchcraft to give to their interiors.

Nurse was in charge of the *lutefisk.* She made a ceremony of preparing the traditional Christmas cod, slowly drying it for days and days before *Jul,* then soaking it in lye until it was swollen to a trembling, jelly-like mass.

Mother Grieg had baked gingerbread and sugar cookies in the form of animals, and several kinds of rich coffee cakes and small cakes. These would be served for the entire *Jul* season (which lasted until January 13) to friends and neighbors who called and to the family at mealtimes.

John and Edvard had attended to the sheaves of wheat for the birds. The grain was placed on spruce poles with enough foliage left to give the birds protection from the wind and wet snow and to provide foothold while they

ate the *Jul* offering. All over Bergen poles like these were
set out to welcome the birds.

Maren and Ingeborg had decorated the Christmas tree.
It stood in the dining-room behind closed doors, waiting
the moment when its glittering wonders would be revealed to the younger children.

Thoughts of that tree and the presents piled like snow-
drifts under it caused Edvard's attention to waver from
the notes.

"Edvard!" His mother's voice came from the kitchen.
"Fie! Edvard! F sharp, F *sharp*—not F!"

Edvard paused in his playing, surprised. A glance at
the book showed him that sure enough, the note was
written F sharp. A look of wonderment crossed his face.
In later years he told many times how filled with awe he
was at this demonstration of his mother's ear for music.
In properly humble mood he returned to his practicing of
"F sharp, not F."

Meanwhile, Edvard's mother was thinking back to the
time when Edvard, a little fellow of five years, had first
reached up to the keys of the piano. His small hands had
carefully searched for the keys which made the tones most
pleasing to him. Unlike most children, he was not trying
to play a melody. He was searching for chords—first a
third, then a triad, then chords of the fourth, fifth, ninth.
Watching him enjoying harmonies which most children
of his age would have considered discords, his mother
realized that her youngest son had no ordinary musical
ear. Soon afterward she began to give him lessons, taking

pride in the fact that Edvard strode forward like a giant as he conquered the technical difficulties of the piano.

In true Norwegian style, however, neither Edvard nor his mother gave any hint of the pride each felt in the other's knowledge and talent. Generations of Norwegians, forced to live in a land where life was hard among the mountains and fjords, had learned to think much and say little. Farming the scanty patches of rocky soil in the deep, dark valleys, every man, woman, and child had learned to depend on his own courage and energy. Isolated one from the other, people grew accustomed to loneliness and silence. And their children, and their children's children, had made a habit of reserved speech.

Edvard brought his playing abruptly to a close when he heard the front door open and shut and a hearty voice call out, "Hallo! Hallo! And where may everybody be? Where is my family?"

This was the signal for an avalanche of legs and arms from upstairs as Maren, Ingeborg, and Elisabeth, Edvard's sisters, and John, his brother, descended by steps or banister to greet their father. Edvard was already perched on his father's shoulders by the time the others arrived, and Mother Grieg was making good-natured scolding noises from the kitchen doorway.

The father of the family, a bluff, hearty man with eyes that sparkled as if he enjoyed a perpetual joke on the world, moved with all his children clinging to him like barnacles to a whale toward the kitchen. He greeted his wife affectionately. Mother Grieg was somewhat embarrassed by what she considered an almost public display of affection, with what the children and Nurse and the rosy-cheeked maid all present. She pushed fussily at her hair and apron to hide her confusion, and hastened to ask questions.

"How was the trip? A good crossing, I hope. The channel was not too rough?"

"Never had a better trip in my life. London is as noisy and gay as ever, business was good, I bought a new volume of Dickens, I heard some fine music, and I brought presents for all of you! How is that for a report, eh?"

Edvard wriggled down from his perch and flew into the hallway where his father's leather traveling bags stood wet from the soft snow which was making this a white Christmas in Bergen. "Come," he called to the others. "Let's open the cases and see what our presents are."

"Oh, no you don't!" His mother appeared on the scene to put a speedy end to this plan. "Your father must be hungry and tired. And it's nearly time for the five o'clock bells to ring." These were the church bells which officially ushered in *Jul*. "We shall have our meal first, and then your father will give you your presents in a civilized manner. Come, all of you," she called to the excited group around Father Grieg. "Time to wash up. And hurry. Nurse and Ingrid and I have prepared a surprise dessert for you."

Mother's word was law in the Grieg household. The children climbed the stairs immediately to tidy up for mealtime. Maren and Ingeborg, the two elder sisters, suddenly remembered that they were almost young ladies.

Maren was fifteen and Ingeborg fourteen. They walked sedately at the head of the procession. John, who was three years older then Edvard, took the stairs two at a time. Edvard came behind with his favorite sister Elisabeth, who was two years younger than he and the baby of the family.

Mealtime in the Grieg household was characterized by dignity and ceremony. The family usually sat at the table in the dining-room, where the rows of bright brass and colorful china on shelves and sideboard gave a cheerful look to the formal room. Because of the tree, which was to be a surprise, Mother Grieg had spread the *Jul* Eve meal on the scrubbed pine table in the kitchen. Father Grieg sat at the head of the table, Mother at the foot. The young Griegs waited quietly to be served with the Christmas dish called *mölje,* the rich hot liquid in which the Christmas meats had been cooked. Once the plates were filled, however, everyone joined in the spirited conversation.

The subject of their excited talk this particular evening was England, from which Father Grieg had just returned. He made frequent trips across the channel on business matters.

Strange to say, though one would have looked far to find a more Norwegian family than the Griegs, there were Scottish ancestors on Father Grieg's side. The name had been spelled *Greig* when Edvard's great-grandfather Alexander, merchant of Aberdeen as his father had been before him, was forced to emigrate after the Battle of Culloden. The Scotch Highlanders, supporting the cause of their Bonny Prince Charlie, had lost the decisive battle of Culloden Moor in 1746. They paid dearly for their defeat. Every twentieth soldier taken by the British was hanged and the rest were deported to the Colonies, and every Scottish merchant suffered from discrimination.

When Alexander Greig became a Norwegian citizen, he changed the spelling of his name so that his Norwegian friends would pronounce it correctly. As it stood, they applied the rules of their own language, giving the *I* rather than the *E* full value in pronunciation; only when the E was written last would they forget the *I* and sound only the long *E*.

By 1779 the *Greig* who became *Grieg* had a prosperous lobster-exporting business; his schooners traded with the very country which had forced him to emigrate. The English government even appointed him English Consul in Bergen. Alexander married a Norwegian girl, and they had a son whom they named John. John married Maren Regine Haslund; one of their children was Alexander Grieg, father of Maren and Ingeborg and John and Edvard and Elisabeth, who sat at that moment impatiently waiting for stories of the English journey. Their mother, sitting so straight and prim at the foot of table, was Norwegian through and through. She could trace her proud ancestry as far back as Kjeld Stub, noted seventeenth-century clergyman, warrior, and scientist of Scandinavia.

"Well, my dears," boomed Father Grieg, "I heard the best concert it has been my privilege to hear in London. An enormous success—not an empty seat in the house, not even in the top balcony!"

Mrs. Grieg smiled to herself. Her husband played the

piano and loved music, there was no doubt of that; yet he invariably judged of the success of a concert by the box-office receipts. This was to be a source of secret and not unkindly amusement between Mrs. Grieg and her son Edvard in later years. To them, artists in the true sense of the word, a good performance would still be good if there was no one who paid to hear it.

"What was the program?" inquired Mrs. Grieg.

"Hum. Yes. Have it in a pocket somewhere. Now where— Oh, yes, here it is." Father Grieg, smiling good-naturedly at his grinning family, handed the printed pro-gram to his wife.

"This was a splendid program," said Mother Grieg in an approving manner. "Mozart, Weber, Mendelssohn, and Chopin. How did they like Chopin?"

"Very well, I should think, judging by the cheering. Of course, a few of the old die-hards amongst the critics think him too revolutionary—call him an extreme Roman-ticist, and they seem to think he has played ducks and drakes with harmony."

Edvard listened attentively. Privately he was thinking that Chopin's music, which his mother and her friends sometimes played, was very much to his taste. The Polish folk melodies and the novel harmonies in Chopin's music seemed strange and eccentric to many of his adult con-temporaries; but to the young Edvard Grieg they sounded natural and supremely beautiful.

"Oh, yes. I went up to Aberdeen this time," Father Grieg went on. "I bought a winter suit there—good Scotch tweed to keep out our winter cold. You know,

Aberdeen's climate reminds me a good bit of the climate here, and I've been thinking that Grandfather Alexander didn't change much except his language when he moved from there."

"Well, he surely changed the marriage prospects of the family," laughed Mother Grieg. "The Griegs have been marrying Norwegians ever since his day, and that wouldn't have happened in Aberdeen."

Looking at his blond brood, Father Grieg had to agree that indeed Alexander had changed more than his language and the spelling of his name. These young Griegs were as Norwegian as Bergen's seven hills or the upland *gaards* and pastures of the Jotunheim, "Home of the Giants."

Ingrid brought in the last dish, the surprise that Mother Grieg had promised.

"Risengrynsgröt!" shouted Edvard, and was immediately silenced by a reproving look from his mother.

Risengrynsgröt was a rice porridge, specially spiced for Christmas, cooked with one almond in it. The one who received that almond was, according to an old belief, the one to be first married.

When the pudding had been served, Elisabeth found the almond on her plate. Everyone laughed, and Edvard teased his little sister all through the rest of the meal.

"You just wanted the almond yourself," declared Elisabeth good-naturedly.

When the children's parents had finished their last cup of fragrant coffee, the family assembled outside the dining-room at last. Cries of delight greeted the opening of the doors. A tall fir tree stood beside the sideboard. The tree was lighted by scores of white wax candles. Its fragrant boughs were decorated with gilded nuts, eggshell toys, red apples, and cookie animals.

Nurse and Ingrid were called in to see the packages unwrapped. Books, toys, music racks, sweaters, games, beautiful pieces of porcelain, clocks, books of music, and a score of other things were in the boxes from the foot of the tree. Father Grieg waited till last to bring out his presents.

The gifts from London made everyone happy. Maren and Ingeborg each received a new party dress, made to order from measurements supplied to their father by Mother Grieg, secretly before his departure. John was made happy by a handsome volume of violoncello music. Like Edvard, he was a student of music, and the 'cello was his instrument. For Elisabeth there was a doll, with long brown curls by way of contrast to her own golden locks. For Edvard there were two beautiful volumes of Sir Walter Scott's *Guy Mannering* and *The Heart of Midlothian* in English.

"To teach you a little of our Scottish beginnings," explained his father, "and maybe to teach you a little English, too. And," he went on, seeing that Edvard's face fell at the thought that his gift meant mostly work, "I have an album of music for you. Some songs of Franz Schubert's." Edvard's beaming face was thanks enough.

For Mother there were several gifts—books, a bolt of silk goods for a dress, and the complete score of Mozart's opera *The Magic Flute.* Nurse was not forgotten, nor

Ingrid either. They received material for dresses and stout woolen hose for winter.

Last of all Father Grieg displayed his own treasures: an English pipe, a can of black-looking tobacco, and a leather-bound volume of Dickens' latest work, *David Copperfield*.

"I can hardly wait to begin it," said Father Grieg, holding the book of his favorite author and smiling like a happy child.

After a while Mother Grieg rose with an air of firm resolve. "I must finish the work in the kitchen. We must be ready for *Juldag*. Up to your rooms, children, and clear up the clutter you have left there from your decorating and gift-wrapping. And don't read by that wretched lamp," she commanded her husband.

The children filed out obediently. Father Grieg took his pipe and book to the drawing-room, where Ingrid had laid a fire against the oak log on the hearth.

When he was sure that Mother, who spared everyone but herself, was busy in the kitchen, Edvard stole back to his father in the drawing-room.

"Well, what's this? A Christmas visit?" called Edvard's father from the easy chair where he was smoking.

"I just came to tell you that I have decided what I shall do to make my living," explained Edvard earnestly.

"So? And what profession have you decided on? No, wait! Let me guess. You'll be a sailor."

"No." Edvard shook his head solemnly.

"A fisherman off the Lofoten Isles?"

"No."

"Then I give up. What shall you be?"

"I shall be a parson," announced Edvard, looking his father straight in the eye to observe what effect the announcement would have on him.

It does great credit to Father Grieg's self-control that he did not laugh; for surely there could not have been a more unparsonlike figure than Edvard at that moment, standing with his hands in his pockets, his legs planted firmly wide apart, his snub nose sitting saucily on his round boyish face. Father Grieg did not even smile, but said kindly, "Can you make a sermon?"

Could he? He not only could but did, then and there, using a high-backed chair for a pulpit. He declaimed about obedience for children, and told how serious a matter it was for boys to go late to school, to waste their study time, to stand under water spouts. When he ran out of sermon material, he recited a poem or two, and his father nearly laughed at this point; for the poems were surely not clerical material. Edvard enjoyed himself immensely. Whenever his audience of one showed signs of going to sleep or resuming the reading of Dickens, he raised his voice and thundered out another poem.

In later years Grieg wrote a memoir of the days of his youth. In this autobiographical essay, which he called *My First Success,* he told how for months the idea of being a parson obsessed him. In those days, he wrote, "I had never for a moment thought that I might become an artist. And if the idea did on any occasion cross my mind, I dismissed it instantly as something unattainable—quite unthinkably high. If I was asked what I was going to be,

I answered dutifully, 'A pastor.' Such a black-clad shepherd of souls my imagination furnished with the most
alluring qualifications I could conceive. To be allowed to
preach or discourse to a listening crowd seemed to me a
great thing. . . . And how I declaimed in season and out
of season to my poor parents and brother and sisters! I
could recite all the poems in our reader by heart. And
every day, after dinner, when my father was longing for a
rest in his easy chair, he could get no peace for me, who,
standing behind a chair for a pulpit, went at it irre-
pressibly. I kept my eye on father, who was, to all appear-
ances, dozing. But he couldn't help smiling now and
again. Then I was happy. That was recognition. And how
I could go on plaguing father! 'Oh, just one other little
piece!'—'No, you've done enough now.'—'Just one more!'
— Ah, childish ambition! It knows to a nicety how stimu-
lating is the sensation of making a success."

On this particular night of *Jul,* Mother Grieg came in
from the kitchen to put an end to all piece-speaking and
sermonizing. Calling the rest of the children, she sat
down at the piano. Her strong, skillful fingers struck the
notes of an old carol. The children clustered round her,
singing, and Father Grieg smiled happily at his family
while he kept time by waving his pipe. They sang until it
was time for Elisabeth to set the bowl of porridge for the
Julenisse, the small gnome with a red-pointed cap and a
long flowing beard.

"Now Julenisse will look after us all year long," declared Elisabeth as she set the gift of porridge on the
hearth to keep it warm for the little household gnome.

Chapter Four

When daisies pied and violets blue
And lady-smocks all silver white
And cuckoo-buds of yellow hue
Do paint the meadows with delight. . . .

LOVE'S LABOR'S LOST

$\mathcal{E}$DVARD sat at the piano waiting for the family to finish their dressing. It was St. John's Eve in the year 1853. In accordance with ancient custom the Grieg family were preparing to join with other revelers to celebrate the old Scandinavian Midsummer Eve. The long Norwegian winter of short days and long, cold nights, when it seemed as if the Frost Giants had won in their eternal struggle with Thor, was past. The awakening of spring would be greeted by the people of the Scandinavian countries with joy and thanksgiving.

Sunlight streamed through the parted draperies of the

44

drawing-room, setting fire to a bowl of Iceland poppies on a small table and finding all the gold in Edvard's hair. The sunbeams conferred an air of gaiety on the formal room, with its dark, polished furniture and heavy carpets. This was no ordinary sun, shining in after the dinner hour. It was the sun of the Norwegian summer, of the long days and the light nights. All over Norway the people's mood was gay and exaggerated to match the sunlight.

Edvard was playing no definite study or composition. He was improvising, as he often did when he was alone. Outside of regular practice hours he could moon and dream as much as he chose. His dreaming took the form of little original melodies, never set down, but vanishing as soon as the notes died away on the air.

Dust motes in the sunlight caught his eye. They were elves, he decided, dancing on Midsummer's Eve. He played a bright melody for them, and it seemed to Edvard that the silver specks danced more briskly to his music.

There was a great deal of rushing about. Maren and Ingeborg ran up and down the stairs, looking for misplaced articles of clothing. Mother brushed Elisabeth's hair and saw to it that John wore a wide bow-tie like his father's. She was giving Edvard a last-minute inspection when Father Grieg drove the family carriage round to the door.

Ingrid in her best Sunday costume, with its wide puffed sleeves of finest lawn and bodice heavy with embroidery and beads, flew back and forth between house and carriage, carrying baskets of food. When they were all seated at last, Father flicked his whip and the horses trotted off briskly. Other carriages and hundreds of people on foot were on their way to the hills and the islands off the coast to celebrate the Springtime Eve of St. John.

The Griegs had decided on one of the hilly, heather-covered wooded islands, where a small village would be celebrating the festival of Midsummer Night in the ancient way. Leaving their carriage at a convenient stable near the wharf called *Dokkeskjeret* they transferred their baskets and themselves to two gaily decked rowboats, for hire by sturdy peasant lads out to make a bit of money on the holiday.

The lads set their hands and backs to the task of rowing their passengers across four miles of water as quickly as possible. "The procession will start soon," explained one of the boys. "This will be our last trip before morning." Other boats were making their way toward the island. Singing, laughing passengers waved merrily to the Grieg children.

When their boats beached, Edvard ran ahead toward the cluster of white red-roofed cottages clustered about a trim little church with a spire standing out above all the roofs. A few houses straggled along the village street which connected hamlet and wharf. It seemed to Edvard as if they had run off from the group around the church to meet him and point the way to the main village. People lined the street near the church. The procession was already moving toward the birch-covered hills back of town.

A little girl had been chosen Midsummer Queen. She was a rosy-cheeked, freckle-faced lass in colorful peasant costume. Her light brown hair was crowned with flowers —Iceland poppies, red as the tiled roofs of her village, yellow roses, and honeysuckle. She was about Edvard's age, and she smiled at him from her perch on the little two-wheeled carriage called a *stolkjaerre* pulled by a fawn-colored Norwegian pony with stiff mane and odd slanted eyes.

"See. The Queen is smiling at Edvard. He is surely the favorite one here today," called out John mischievously.

Following their queen came a procession of boys and girls, all with flowers in their hair or caps, and some carrying flowers which they scattered along the way as they walked. At the very end of the line walked the village fiddlers, playing the curious *Hardingfeles*, the native violins of Norway. Steel strings directly under the gut strings vibrate as the bow is drawn across the upper strings, providing a drone bass for the melody. The effect is like the steady drone of the Scotch bagpipe.

"Listen! An old folk melody, which my nurse used to sing to me when I was a child!" Edvard's mother was smiling and nodding her head in time to the odd rhythm of *I Laid Me Down To Rest.*

The whole village and all the visitors from Bergen followed the gay procession up to the hills. The sun was still high in the sky, though it was nearly eight o'clock. This was the Norwegian midsummer. Sunset would not be before ten o'clock in this far northern land, and at midnight there would still be enough light to read a book by.

On top of the highest hill, logs and tar-soaked barrels had been piled in a huge mound. When the sun dropped at last behind the hill, the mound would be lighted to make a St. John's bonfire.

Several hundred people had made their way to the hilltop. There were boys in short sailors' jackets and city youths in the pale green shirts seen everywhere in Bergen. Peasant costumes from Hardanger, with the embroidery for which they were famous all over the world, were much in evidence. Red skirts and black skirts, beaded bodices and high-necked blouses, short trousers and buckled shoes, high-crowned hats and close-fitting caps— costumes from a score of valleys and fjord districts— made merry amongst the more sober clothes of modern cut.

Tablecloths were spread, and each family group unpacked its picnic baskets. The sea air and the climb had given Edvard a good appetite. His mother watched him with pleasure; there were times when she fancied that he was not so strong as the rest of the children. It pleased her to see him eating hungrily. And what a feast it was! Sharp cheese, fish rolled in golden brown bread crumbs, spiced sausages, preserved cherries, and good sweet butter, rye bread in thick slices, bottles of fruit punch made by Mother Grieg herself.

When the sun sank into the sea beyond the hills, a shout went up and the bonfire was lighted immediately. In a few moments twinkling points of light, some of them so far away that they resembled stars, sprang up on the mainland and on the many islands dotting the coastline.

The fiddlers struck up a wild tune and the costumed peasants began a dance around the fire.

Father Grieg chuckled to himself. "We are still a pagan people, I'm afraid. In just this way our Viking ancestors ushered in the spring, celebrating the summer solstice. Though these dancers do not know it, I'll be bound, they are really dancing the votive dance to Freya, goddess of fertility. The fires were originally beacon fires to communicate from place to place the directions of the pagan priests concerning agriculture and fishing."

"But why is it called St. John's Eve?" Edvard and Elisabeth wanted to know.

"Well, you see, even St. Olaf with his trusty sword found it hard to drive out the old pagan customs. So the Church decided to abolish the old pagan customs gradually. It let the people have their Midsummer's Eve fires and dances. It explained, however, that the old pagan meaning of the celebration had been changed, that they were really celebrating the nativity of St. John Baptist. And for a time I suspect that some of the people celebrated St. John and some just kept on celebrating Freya. But the result was about the same. There were bonfires and fiddle music and dancing, no matter what the celebration meant to the dancers."

It was long after midnight when the Griegs found their peasant lads again and arranged to return to the mainland. It was dark at last, and the stars twinkled brightly in the northern sky.

"They look like St. John's bonfires, too," said Edvard sleepily. Over the water came the sound of singing and shouting. The revelers would not stop their dancing until the dawn had ushered in St. John's Day.

"It was to celebrate such a night as this—at Queen Elizabeth's court in England, perhaps—that William Shakespeare, nearly two hundred and fifty years ago, wrote his play called *A Midsummer Night's Dream*," said Father Grieg when they were in their carriage once more.

As the horses jogged along homeward, Edvard listened drowsily to his father reciting a fairy song from that fanciful play:

> "Over hill, over dale,
>   Thorough bush, thorough brier,
> Over park, over pale,
>   Thorough flood, thorough fire,
> I do wander everywhere,
>   Swifter than the moonës sphere;
> And I serve the fairy queen,
> To dew her orbs upon the green:
> The cowslips tall her pensioners be;
> In their gold coats spots you see;
> These be rubies, fairy favours,
> In their freckles live their savours:
> I must go seek some dewdrops here,
> And hang a pearl in every cowslip's ear."

That was all that Edvard remembered that night. Next morning he woke in his little room far out in Strandgaten to find that dewdrops had been flung into all the flower cups of the garden. Nurse was calling him to breakfast, and outside in the vines some birds were making a noisy clatter, chattering, no doubt, about the best places for their nests that year.

Chapter Five

Merrily, merrily shall I live now
Under the blossom that hangs on the bough.
THE TEMPEST

$\mathcal{J}$HE year 1858 marked a turning point in Edvard's life. In the spring of that year he wound up his studies at the local school and never returned as a student to its stuffy halls. In the fall, an opportunity came to him which at first seemed as unreal as a dream and was to settle the matter of his future for good and all. But between spring and fall he spent the summer of his fifteenth year enjoying a carefree vacation at Rissen village on Trondhjem Fjord.

Edvard had accompanied his father several times in past summers on the little coastwise mailboats plying between Bergen and the ports north of Trondhjem. The leisurely voyage, with the boats putting in often to unload mail at ports of the mainland or the myriads of islands to the west, was always a new adventure.

The trip north in 1858 was no exception. The bright sky of the Norwegian summer was no gayer than the spirits of Edvard and his father when, shortly after celebrating Edvard's birthday, the two of them stood at the rail of the Trondhjem mail steamer and watched Bergen's wooded hills recede in the distance.

"I want you to stay outdoors as much as possible this summer," Edvard's father told him.

Though Father and Mother Grieg did not say so, they were often concerned over Edvard's health. A winter of school and music seemed to tire him too much. They were hoping that living the sturdy, simple life of the peasants at Rissen would bring the color back to their youngest son's pale cheeks.

Edvard stayed on deck every evening until the last rays of the late-setting sun faded from the sky and the color in the hollows of the waves changed from gold to ultramarine. He found much to interest him as the boat glided on its way past desolate rocky shores, mysterious islands where the sea gulls cried raucously, and lonely farmhouses clinging precariously to cliffs falling sheer to the sea. The boat put in often at fishing villages, with snow-capped mountains at their back and rugged foothills so close that sometimes they seemed to be crowding the rickety frame houses and piers into the water.

At the entrance to the Sognefjord, where the welcome darkness descended for a few hours of the summer night, phosphorescent jellyfishes made an eerie light on the calm water. Edvard thought of the stories of the will-o'-the-wisp lamps of the trolls and the hobgoblins said to lead travelers astray on the mountain heights. Those lights would be like these—spectral, blue, cold.

Northward from the Sognefjord their boat made its way in the calm waters of the Skjåergard, past the island of Bremanger where gray, bare Hornelen, the highest sea cliff in Europe, rose almost straight up from the water's edge. As the boat passed under Hornelen's over-hanging summit, the sea birds, disturbed in their lonely heights, set up a din of screaming and mournful crying.

"They say that King Olaf Trygvason climbed that rock in the year 1000," Edvard's father told him as the ship went on its way past the entrance to the Nord Fjord.

At the little town of Molde, the passengers landed for a few hours. Edvard always loved the quaint quay of Molde, where gabled houses leaned toward the wharf. He and his father took their midday meal in the town itself, at a picturesque little inn commanding a view of the fjord and the distant snow-peaked mountains. Everywhere there grew on the hills a profusion of roses and honeysuckle. Beside the farm buildings and along the streets such trees as the ash, horse-chestnut, lime and beech thrived because of the sheltered location which gives Molde a temperate climate and the look of a more southern land.

"We shall spend a day or so at Trondhjem," said Edvard's father. "You are so fond of Olaf Trygvason, you ought to get to know his capital well."

Together, Edvard and his father explored the broad

streets of Munkegate and Kongensgate, and visited the
busy market-place of Trondhjem. They walked along
tree-lined avenues to the old cathedral, which in the days
of its glory boasted 3,360 pillars, 316 windows filled
with stained glass from Cologne, and beautiful frescoes
along its walls. Fire and pillaging and the plague had
done their work. The cathedral was in need of restoration. But its high towers, made of the dove-gray soap-
stone from the quarries east of Trondhjem and marble
from the island of Almenningen, looked out proudly
over fjord and sea.

Thinking of St. Olaf and Trygvason brought a lump
to Edvard's throat. Grandfather Hagerup, who had first
told him the story of the two great Vikings, had died
five years before, when Edvard was not quite ten. The
memory of his passing was still a poignant memory. As
if it had been yesterday, Edvard remembered the elaborate funeral, almost barbaric in its pomp and splendor.
The funeral march which accompanied the proud old
Stiftamtmann to the grave made so deep an impression
on Edvard that parts of it persisted in repeating their
mournful phrases to his inner ear for years afterward.

At Rissen village, Edvard's father left his son to board
with a peasant family. All that summer, Edvard wore
the rough clothes and did the hard work of a peasant
lad. Early in the summer, he helped with mending the
fish nets, tarring the boats, and mending the lines. Sometimes he went out with the men to set the long lines for
the catch.

When the farmers in the little *gaards* above town needed help later in the summer, he took his turn at the scything of hay, and helped to hang it on the racks built like fences. In a land of frequent rain, hay must be hung up to dry like clothes on a line.

Toward the end of the summer he went with one of the fishermen to the Iskoe fair. They went by boat up Trondhjem Fjord, Edvard taking his turn at the oars. Jagged cliffs rose on either side of the winding fjord. Sometimes there were turns in the course of the fjord so sharp that Edvard was sure that the way was blocked by the black cliffs. But beyond the turns the waterway always extended green and cool before them.

At one point the cliffs came so close together that they threw a perpetual shadow on the water. High overhead a narrow slit of bright sky was all there was to tell that the sun still shone. Cascades of water poured over the lichen-covered cliffs, and beyond were the mountains with belts of fir trees and above the fir belt the lighter green of the birches. Above all, the perpetual snows glistened.

Here and there, where the glaciers of the ice age had scraped a hollow or made a ledge in the sheer cliff walls, a little farm clung to its patch of earth. Goats were tethered, and small children too, to keep them from falling out of the slanting yards into the thousand-foot-deep fjord below. Gulls wheeled overhead. Their cries were as strange and lonely as the fjord itself.

Distant musical notes caused Edvard to sit up straight and listen. "What is that?" he asked the fisherman.

"That? Oh, that must be a *lur,* the horn used here-abouts for calling the cattle and the goats," explained his companion.

"How I should like to see the *lur* played! Do you suppose we might stop and climb up to where the shepherd is?"

"Ho! Listen to the lad! Why, that horn we just heard may be miles away. The *lur* makes a powerful sound and carries far—and it takes lungs like leather bellows to blow it."

Again the minor notes of the *lur* sounded. Edvard fell to picturing to himself the lonely shepherd standing beside the *saeter* (temporary farm shelter), sounding the horn for his own amusement, possibly, to make the silence of the upland pastures less depressing.

The village of Iskoe was situated on a sloping bank of the fjord, with the mountain called Trolltinder looming beyond. These jagged peaks, known as the Haunted Mountains throughout Scandinavia, were said to be the home of a witch woman, the *Gefu,* whose trolls and witch companions gave rewards to the fair and honor-able and punished the disagreeable and dishonest.

"Most of the villagers," laughed Edvard's fisherman friend, who was a man who had been south by sea to Bergen and knew a thing or two, "Most of the villagers believe that something terrible will happen to them if they build a home even on the Gefu's foothill domain. They shun the Trolltinder mountain, I can tell you."

The Iskoe fair was in full swing when Edvard and his companion arrived. The fisherman immediately set out to find a place where he could display his wares. He had brought carved wooden objects made by his crippled father during the long winter months.

Edvard wandered about, studying the people from the farms and villages. Peasant women and girls in short skirts and bright bodices, men and boys wearing short trousers and brief jackets made up the gay crowds. Some were selling, some buying the trinkets and useful articles displayed at the market-place. There were carved wooden toys, nutcrackers, salad bowls, delicate lace work made by gnarled hands, woolen shawls from the hand looms of the valleys. There were piles and barrels of food, too —rye bread heaped up on the scrubbed tables, cheese, fresh butter, eggs, chickens, and fish. In the air hung a smell of coffee, kept simmering for those who wanted to eat Norwegian rolls and coffee breads.

A group of young people surrounded a boy playing a shepherd's pipe. Edvard joined them, admiring the shepherd's agile fingers. A tall, broad-shouldered man walked up beside him. Looking up, Edvard met the bluest, most twinkling eyes he had ever seen. The stranger smiled at him and spoke in a hearty voice. "You ought to hear the pipes I have at my home on Trolltinder!"

Edvard's eyes opened wide. "You are Olaf the Lucky!" Everyone who had ever visited the Trondhjem region knew about Norway's most famous sailor, who had been all over the world, and who had settled down at last on one of the slopes of the Haunted Mountains with all the treasures of his wanderings.

"Would you like to come up to my place and see some of my pipes and flutes?" was the tall man's next surprising utterance.

Edvard lost no time in telling his fisherman friend of his plans to go with Olaf.

"We'd better sing the Gefu song on the way home," said Olaf, quite seriously. "You see, I live on what is considered her land. I always sing the 'lucky song' to please the old witch when I go home." With this explanation, the tall sailor boomed out in his hearty voice the strange folk song which is said to placate the Gefu. He continued singing till he was on his own door mat.

Olaf's house was a cozy wooden farmhouse. Its main room, with fireplace and huge table, was littered with objects from the journeys around the world. There were carved chests from China, Samurai swords obtained from Japan when that land was still closed to the trade of the world, idols from the Malay jungles, a necklace of human teeth from Borneo, a beautiful lace mantilla from Cadiz, a walrus tusk from the Norwegian Sea far to the north.

Olaf had a collection of all sorts of musical instruments. He took them from their shelves and showed Edvard how they were played. There was a *lur* in the collection, made of wood with birchbark covering. Putting the long horn to his lips, Olaf sounded a blast that Edvard thought must have been heard down in Trondhjem itself.

While Edvard was still at Olaf's place, the sky darkened with thunder clouds. Jagged lightning split the sky over the wild cliffs and mountain tops, and thunder rolled and rumbled.

"Thor is throwing his hammer about," smiled Olaf.

"And I must go. My friend will worry," said Edvard.

Running through the pastures toward the village, Edvard sniffed the rain-laden air and took off his cap to let the damp breeze ruffle his hair. He paused to send a last farewell shout to tall Olaf standing in his doorway, and Olaf sent after him a huge bellowing that rivaled Thor's hammer.

It was late when Edvard and his friend returned to Rissen that night. The good fisherfolk with whom Edvard stayed had been worried. They chided him gently and set out a warmed-over meal for him.

"And we saved you some of your favorite—*rodgrot!*" said the fisherman's wife. "You're treated better than you deserve to be, though, with your wild wandering ways as if you were a shepherd lad daft from loneliness."

Edvard plunged an eager fork into the barley flour stewed with blueberries, topped with sugar syrup and thick cream. This was the Norwegian dish of *rodgrot.* For Edvard there would be few things that tasted better.

Lying on his back one day under an oak tree whose leaves were turning red from the early frosts, Edvard watched the clouds piling themselves into fantastic shapes in the pale blue sky. His thoughts were as vague as the outlines of the seed pods in their summer down floating in the breeze. A light tap on the shoulder brought him to earth.

"Time to go home, Edvard, lad." It was the kindly voice of the old fisherman with whom he boarded. "The cart will be ready in an hour to take your trunk to the boat."

The summer at Rissen was over.

Chapter Six

Everything that heard him play,
Even the billows of the sea,
Hung their heads, and then lay by.

HENRY VIII

RETURNING to Bergen in the fall, Edvard joined his family at Landås, the pleasant country estate left to them after Grandfather Hagerup's death.

The days were shorter, and autumn's frosty breath had turned the trees to flaming torches and golden beacons when the important event of Grieg's early life occurred. Ole Bull came riding up to Landås one afternoon.

Ole Bull was Norway's greatest violinist. Some called him the greatest violinist of all time, not excluding his famous teacher Paganini. Ole Bull was the first great artist to appreciate fully the value of the Norse folk music. This music, together with his own compositions inspired by nature impressions in his native land, he had taken out to the world, so that all might appreciate the great contribution of the Norwegian fiddlers.

Edvard like every other citizen of Bergen, which was Ole Bull's birthplace, had heard exciting stories of the great artist's adventures in America and other parts of the world. When he was told that the tall, flaxen-haired Viking dismounting in their dooryard was Ole Bull, Edvard's heart beat with jubilation. His eyes searched eagerly for a black case. How he was wishing that Ole Bull had brought the famous Stradivarius violin with its almost flat bridge and exquisite ivory and ebony inlay! It was told that "Norse Ole" with his heavy bow could bring magic song learned from the water nix from that violin. But Ole Bull had come without his fiddle that day.

"Welcome to Landås," boomed Father Grieg, opening the door to his illustrious guest. "I almost said, 'Welcome home.' You have been a stranger to us for the last few years, staying in America as you have been."

"Yes, I have had to stay away from my dear Westland more than has been good for me."

"Or for us, dear Ole Bull." Edvard's mother spoke from the door of the drawing-room. "Please come in. I want you to meet my youngest son—Edvard. He studies piano."

"Good, good." Ole Bull had a jovial, friendly manner that seemed to fill a whole room with warmth and gaiety. "You must play something for me before I go, Edvard."

Edvard smiled and said he would, but he turned quite pale at the thought of performing before one of the

greatest musicians of the world. He was glad when
Father Grieg delayed the playing by calling for wine and
cakes for his guest. Ole Bull seated his long, lithe figure
in the deepest chair in the room and began to talk as only
he could.

Edvard, sitting in an obscure corner, listened to Bull's
anecdotes and his jokes with a feeling of surprise and
some disappointment. Instead of being the strange, super-
natural sort of creature Edvard had come to believe him,
he was just a Norwegian like Edvard himself, fanciful
and serious by turns, kindly and human. Mother Grieg
smiled at her son, as if she had guessed his thoughts and
wanted to say, "Isn't he better this way? Would you
have wanted him to be a troll or a giant or an elf-man?
Ole Bull is one of us."

Ole Bull was speaking of his trials and tribulations in
managing the Norse Theater, which he had established
in Bergen eight years before. This theater had in 1851
given an almost starving young man of twenty-three a job;
that man was Henrik Ibsen, who became the greatest play-
wright of his time. Another great writing name came to
be associated with Ole Bull's theater, that of Björnstjerne
Björnson. Both these men were to play an important part
in Edvard Grieg's career, though there was no hint of
that on the autumn afternoon when Ole Bull sat chatting
at Landås.

He was describing the opening of his theater, where
he had hoped to see performed all the great folk dramas
and folk music of his country. "The opening performance
was really an historic event," said Bull, his eyes lighting

at the memory. "The great Möllargutten played the old
tunes on his *hardingfele*. He was a dear friend, old
Möllargutten. His true name was Thorgeir Audunsön of
Haukelid-Rock. I knew him when I was a boy. How
many times have I heard him play at weddings and festivals in the country districts!

"I can close my eyes and see the dances as they were
performed by lusty peasant couples. The *halling*, especially. As it commences it is slow, almost majestic, and
the forms of the dancers move with grace and dignity.
Gradually the music becomes quicker. Faster and faster
dances the fiddler's bow across the gut strings. The steel
strings beneath set up a powerful humming. The halling
turns into a leaping dance. Only the strongest young men
can stay on the floor. Each tries to outdo the others, leaping in his efforts to kick the ceiling.

"Fierce and wild and free was Thorgeir in those days,
and his fiddle an instrument bewitched. Some of the old
people whispered that he had learned his art from the
green-haired nix who lived in the waterfall by his mill.
They had no doubt that he had bartered his soul for the
magic eleventh tune.

"Well, of course I thought first of all of Thorgeir
when I set about organizing the Norse Theater. I sent
word to him to come and help me on the first night. I
didn't know whether he would or not; for he was a shy
man in the city. But it seems he remembered the boy Ole,
who had learned a trick or two from watching the nimble
fingers and stout bowing arm of 'the miller.' He came at
once. I heard later how as he rode through the lonely

country districts people tried to persuade him to stop and play for their dances; but Thorgeir stubbornly shook his old head and said, 'Ole expects me at the Norse Theater.'

"I shall never forget his playing that first night at the theater. Even our Bergen audience, who for the most part had been brought up to believe that there was no culture in their native land, that their language must be Danish and their music German or French, sat up and took notice.

"One of the pieces Thorgeir played was closely connected with an old ballad of his native district: A pretty young girl met the elf-king, the story goes. He sang so enchantingly to her that she followed him to a mountain, which opened to receive them and then closed. Hearing the girl's calls for help, her father hastened to the mountain, but his daughter told him there was no hope for her unless he could bring the village bell from the steeple and set it to ringing before sunset. This great task her father hastened to perform. With the aid of the entire village, he hauled the heavy bell to the mountain, but the rope broke just as the sun was setting and the girl's voice was still forever.

"Will you believe me that Möllargutten's fiddle told all that? It snarled with the triumphant exulting of the demon-king. It wailed and sobbed and yearned tenderly after the lost girl. The music died away in tearless mourning, bitter and hopeless."

"And then I suppose the old miller went home," said Edvard suddenly.

"I see you know the peasant character well," smiled

Ole Bull. "Where else would he go? How out of place
he would have been in our city! He belonged to the
mountains and lonely farms and the dark rock of Hauke-
lid. Yes, he went home, taking with him 2,000 specie
dollars, and a pair of shoes, and a silk neckerchief for
his wife. You know, I once heard Thorgeir say that his
great ambition was to buy a pair of shoes and a silk ker-
chief for his wife. Somehow, I think he must have been
the happiest man in the world. There are not many who
achieve their life's ambition so surely and simply as he
did." Whimsically, Ole Bull raised his glass high as a
toast to his old friend, the miller of Haukelid-Rock.

"Are they true, these stories we hear about your adventures in America?" Father Grieg wanted to know.

"Well," laughed Ole Bull, "I don't know what you
may have heard. But it is true that I have had some hair-
raising encounters in the rough Far West and in the Ohio
and Mississippi river country.

"Once when I was going down the Mississippi on a
steamboat, a party of men, colonists to the West, came up
to me and offered me a drink of the raw whisky which
had already made them quarrelsome.

" 'I thank you,' I said, 'but I never drink whisky.'

"With an ugly leer, one of the men asked me if I was
a 'teetotaler.' I judged from his tone that there was nothing worse in his estimation.

" 'No,' I said. 'I like a glass of wine, but whisky is like
poison to me.'

"Then my tormentor shouted, 'If you can't drink, you

must fight!' And all the rest of his crowd set up a din, shouting, 'You look strong; show us what you are good for!'

"It was clear that they thought my fiddle-playing a poor excuse for my existence.

" 'Well,' I said, 'a Norseman can fight as well as anybody when his blood is up, but my blood is cold, and why should I?'

"They began to get quite ugly; so I said, 'Since you insist, I will tell you what I will do. Let any one of you take hold of me in any way he likes, and I'll wager that in half a minute he shall lie on his back at my feet.'

"A big fellow was chosen to make the test. He stepped up, grabbed my waist, and before he could change the tobacco in his mouth from cheek to cheek, he was lying senseless on the deck. For the next moment or so I was pretty uncomfortable. Out of the corner of my eye I saw one of the man's comrades draw a bowie knife, a murderous-looking weapon. I drew a sigh of relief, I can tell you, when I saw him use the knife to open a flask. A good dose of liquor was poured down the throat of the vanquished gladiator. His first question, which aroused much amusement, was 'How did I get down here? What in blazes hit me?'

"He laughed ruefully when he realized that I, a mere musician, was responsible for his plight. He shook hands and insisted that I take his knife as a gift. 'Take it home with you,' he said. 'You fight better than Mike, the Cock o' the Walk. You're as quick as lightnin'.'"

Ole Bull stayed for dinner. Edvard listened with the

rest to the tales this odd musician had to tell. Ole Bull said very little of the bitter days in Paris, when he was a struggling and starving young artist; but he did speak of the days of his boyhood.

"Do you know," he said, smiling his gentle smile, "when I was a little chap—about three years old—I discovered a bluebell in the meadow. It nodded in the breeze, and I actually imagined I heard it ringing. I said so at home, and got a spanking for telling falsehoods. It was Uncle Jens who realized that all this rigmarole I was forever telling about hearing bluebells ring and the grasses play music was my inner ear hearing the melodies played at his home. He bought me a violin, yellow as a lemon, and made me blissfully happy by allowing me to join in the ensemble playing at his house."

Then there was the tale about the old recluse who lived at the edge of town. Strange stories were told about this old fellow, and Ole Bull had come to fear him. Whenever he had to pass the house where the man lived, Ole would run as fast as his legs would carry him. What was his horror one day, then, to hear his name called as he hurried by the dreaded house. The old man was standing by the gate of his little garden. "Come in," he called. "I have a fiddle I bought in England. Come see it."

Ole's heart was in his mouth, but he followed the recluse into the cottage. Fear left him as he studied the old man's face, which had a wistful but kindly expression. The fiddle proved to be an old instrument, in need of a sound post. Ole was told that he might whittle out the missing part. When the post was adjusted and the strings tuned, Ole tried the frayed bow. The old man listened eagerly to the Norwegian folk dances which Ole played with ease and charm.

"Can you play *God Save the King?*" the old man inquired.

"Yes, I can play it." Ole brightened the hymn-like tune with fanciful variations, presenting the simple melody in twenty different ways.

There were tears in the old man's eyes when he bade Ole goodbye. "You must come again," he said. "You have made me almost happy again."

As Ole walked away, he heard the cooing of doves from a cote at the back of the garden. The old recluse stood at the gate, watching his young friend out of sight.

The following afternoon, toward dusk, the doorbell rang at Ole Bull's house. When his mother answered the ring, she was surprised to find only a basket on the doorstep. The basket contained four pairs of doves—very rare and very beautiful doves—a present from the lonely old man whose favorite tune was *God Save the King.*

Edvard grinned when Ole Bull told them that he had found school very dull.

"My father thought I might do better under the supervision of a private tutor," said Bull. "So he hired a Mr. Musaeus. He was a learned man, but a creature of absolutely berserk rages." Ole Bull went on to tell how he had taught this sadistic teacher a lesson. He had Edvard and Mother and Father Grieg shaking with laughter before the tale was done.

It seems that cross words and blows from Mr. Musaeus

were all too frequent during study hours. Finally Ole
Bull and his brothers decided that matters had been carried too far. The stern discipline of those days made them
hesitate to carry tales to their father. If Musaeus was to
be taught a lesson, they must do it themselves.

Ole, who had developed into a strong, athletic boy,
was naturally the leader in the undertaking. All the boys
were lying awake one morning, awaiting their tutor,
whose greatest delight was to drag the youngest one
roughly from his warm bed at four o'clock in the
morning.

At the moment Musaeus laid hand on the bed-covers,
Ole sprang on his back with a growl. The tutor was no
match for the lithe Ole, and soon went down helpless on
the floor. Truth to tell, the younger brothers had promised to help overpower the tutor, but they only covered
up their heads during the struggle, uncovering them now
and then to cry, "Don't give up, Ole! Don't give up!
Give it to him with all your might!"

The whole household below stairs was roused. A terrified maid and the boys' mother appeared at the same
moment, and Ole's father was close behind them. Ole
expected an angry rebuke from his father and mother,
but they merely exchanged an amused look. They had
begun to realize that their tutor was hardly the ideal
employee.

"That will do now, Ole," was all that his father said
on the subject.

Edvard, thinking of his own schooldays, was wishing
that he had been strong enough to thrash the teacher the

day that stern schoolmaster pulled his hair until everything went black before his eyes. Edvard was just twelve
when that happened. He had made his first attempt at
composition—*Variations on a German Melody* he called
his work. He had brought it proudly to school to show
it to a classmate. The classmate, bursting with pride at
his chum's achievement, had blurted out in class time,
"Edvard has something!"

"Something? What do you mean?" demanded the
teacher.

"Grieg has composed something!"

In later years, Grieg wrote an account of what followed:

"The teacher, with whom for the very good reasons I
have described I was not at all popular, got up, came
over to me, looked at the sheet of music and said in a
characteristically ironical but not ungracious tone: 'So—
so, the young rascal is musical—the young rascal com-
poses. Let's have a look at this!' With which he opened
the door to the next classroom, brought the teacher from
it in to us and went on: 'Just look at this—that young
scamp there is a composer.' Both teachers turned over the
pages of my music with interest. There was general excitement in both classes. I felt myself already sure of a
great success. But one mustn't be too confident. For no
sooner was the visitor gone than our own teacher suddenly changed his tactics, grabbed me by the hair, so that
everything went black before my eyes, and snapped
abruptly: 'Another time he will have the German dictionary with him as he should and leave such trash at

home.' Oh, misery! So near the peak of happiness and then in a moment down in the depths! How often has it been like that for me in life. And every time my thoughts have gone back involuntarily to this first time."

In that same memoir of the days of his boyhood, Edvard Grieg told how he played for Ole Bull at Landås and what came of that event:

"When he got to know that I was keen on composing and improvising, there was no saying him nay: I must to the piano. I do not understand what Ole Bull could find at that time in my naïve childish notes, but he grew serious and talked in a low voice with my parents. The result of this discussion was not to my disadvantage. For suddenly Ole Bull came over to me, shook me in his own characteristic fashion and said: 'You are to go to Leipzig and become a musician.' Everyone looked at me affectionately, but I grasped only one thing, that a kind fairy was stroking my cheek and that I was happy. And my parents! Not a moment's opposition nor even hesitation. Everything was decided. And I thought it all the most natural thing in the world and did not realize till long afterwards all the gratitude I owed to my parents and to Ole Bull. The spirit of adventure had cast its spell upon me and nothing else could move me."

Thus it was that Edvard changed his mind about becoming a pastor, and dedicated himself to music instead.

Chapter Seven

Jog on, jog on, the footpath way,
And merrily hent the stile-a:
A merry heart goes all the day,
Your sad tires in a mile-a.

A WINTER'S TALE

VERY soon after Ole Bull's visit to Landås, preparations were made to send Edvard to the Conservatory of
Leipzig, which had been founded by Mendelssohn in
1843, the year of Edvard's birth. From all over the con-
tinent and from the British Isles, young musicians came
to this great school to study with its professors, the greatest musical men of their time.

When young Grieg's application had been accepted
by the Director of the Conservatory, Edvard and his
father made ready in the late fall of 1858 to leave Bergen.
Their journey would be a matter of many days. They
planned to go overland to Christiania (modern Oslo);
from there they would take ship across the Skagerrak

and down the Kattegat to Copenhagen in Denmark. And
then the way would lie over the North Sea to the German
seaport of Hamburg.

Bundled up warmly against the nippy fall air, Edvard
and his father waved goodbye from their *stolkjaerre* to
Mother Grieg and Maren, Ingeborg, Elisabeth, and John.
Maren and Ingeborg called well-meant advice after
Edvard. John, already feeling it a duty to put aside his
'cello in favor of a business career, looked wistfully after
his brother. Elisabeth, the youngest sister, wiped her red
eyes. She had been weeping because life promised to be
lonely and dull without her favorite brother as companion.

The little Norwegian cart and strong young pony,
rented for the trip to Sognefjord, moved briskly over the
pleasant country lanes and rocky hillside roads skirting
the shoreline.

Edvard, as he sat watching Bergen's heather-clad hills
and wooded heights fading into the distance, had his first
premonitions that his adventure might not always be gay
and heedless.

"Well, Edvard, lad, you're on your way to being a
musician. Does it make you happy?"

"Yes, but a little sad, too," admitted Edvard truthfully.
"I shall miss the family."

"Nonsense! You're not a baby, you know. No homesickness, now. I'll wager we shall be more lonely than
you. You will have friends and companions. The students
of Germany are a merry lot. You will be singing through
the streets and carrying a torch in the midnight proces-

sions and dancing around bonfires with the best of them, never fear."

His father's words drove away the doubts which had clutched at Edvard for a moment. Presently, he was his usual sunny, optimistic self.

"How far shall we go today?" he asked, thinking of the wonderful journey ahead of them over the high plateau and mountain region of Norway.

"Oh, we'll stop at some village just this side of the Sogne. I'll arrange to send our cart and pony back to Bergen and make enquiries about a boat to take us up the Sognefjord."

In the cart was a basket of lunch for the travelers. They made a picnic of the midday meal, spreading it out in a sunny place protected from the freshening west wind by a clump of rowan trees and bird cherry.

That night they put up at a farmhouse in a village a half-day's trip to the Sogne. Edvard's father arranged with the farmer to haul them and their baggage next day to the fjord. A village boy was only too eager to make a little money and have a trip to Bergen into the bargain —and so the *stolkjaerre* was sent back to its owner in the city.

The trip up Sognefjord as far as Laerdalsöyri was made in easy stages by rowboat. Edvard and his father beached their little craft often on the shores of the tiny islands that dotted the great fjord. They would rest for a while and enjoy the majestic scenery of Norway's deepest and longest arm of the sea. Edvard knew that to the north lay the glaciers of the Jostedalsbrae snowfield, and that Fresviksbrae with its ice cap rose nearer at hand. But steep cliffs enclosed the fjord to make a narrow world of water only. These cliffs were black lava, glistening green where cascades fell from tree-crowned summits to meet the salt fjord.

Where the Sogne widened, black, sheer cliffs gave way to fine sweeps of rolling, pasture-clad hills and wooded slopes facing to the south. The days were becoming short, and when night overtook the two boatmen, they beached their craft and climbed to one of the farmhouses high on one of these lonely hills. They were always made welcome, fed with good bread and cheese, and butter fresh from the churning. At one such stopping place they found themselves in the midst of a peasant wedding celebration. Neighbors from the village back from the Sogne had assembled with presents and *hardingfeles*. That night Edvard snuggled into a feather-bed in the loftlike upper room provided for him and his father, and fell asleep to the plaintive minors of old folk tunes played below by the fiddlers.

From Laerdalsöyri they traveled on horseback across the mountains. For the first time, Edvard was seeing part of the great Jotunheim of Norway—the Home of the Giants. To his left as his horse trotted on toward the Valdres Valley, he saw the crowns of Glittertind and majestic Galdhöpiggen, highest mountains in Europe north of the Carpathians. This journey took them past beetling cliffs, over high mountain passes bare of timber, where the wind whistled perpetually, sweeping down from the glaciers to the west and north. Lower down their horses followed ancient paths in the forests fragrant with the scent of fir and pine. The towering snowcaps of the main range looked like clouds where they touched the pale blue sky. The impression that the Jotunheim region made on Edvard was deep and lasting. In later years, he made almost annually a trip into the bracing air of this high region, and the nature impressions he gathered there went into his great music.

As they walked to rest their horses, Edvard's father told one of the old stories about Thor and the Giants who were supposed to live in Jotunheim.

"The giant Thrym stole Thor's hammer and carried it off to Jotunheim. So great was Thor's rage on discovering the theft that he walked up and down, shaking his red beard, and with every step he caused the valleys to tremble and the high peaks to topple.

"When Loki was told what had happened, he sought out Freya, borrowed her feather dress, which enabled its wearer to fly through the air with the speed of the wind, and flew to Jotunheim. There Thrym, lord of the giants, sat on a mound, making golden leashes for his dogs and stroking the manes of his huge horses.

"Loki cried out: 'Bold Thrym, Lord of the Giants, thou hast a visitor.'

"Thrym answered, 'How fares it with gods and elves? Why comest thou alone to Jotunheim?'

" 'Ill fares it with gods and elves,' replied Loki. 'Where hast thou hidden Thor's hammer?'

" 'In the Jotunheim, eight miles deep,' said Thrym. 'And none shall have it unless I am given Freya for bride.'

"Loki flew back with these tidings, and he and Thor sought out Freya. Loki commanded her to put on a bridal veil and hasten to Jotunheim. But Freya had other ideas. So great was her anger that the dwelling in which the gods stood was shaken and Freya's necklace, called Brisinga, of which she was so proud, broke. Freya won the argument and the rest of the gods met in council to see what might be done.

"Heimdall advised Thor to go to Jotunheim disguised as Freya. After some protest, Thor was persuaded that this was the only way he could get his hammer back; so the huge god of war put on a veil, woman's dress, head-gear, and necklace, and hung keys at his girdle. Loki attended him disguised as a maidservant.

"In Thor's goat-chariot they hastened to Jotunheim, their speed causing the mountains to burst and blaze with fire. Thrym received them without suspicion. He ordered a feast prepared. To Thrym's amazement, Thor, the glut-tonous eater amongst the gods, ate an ox, a salmon, and all the dainties provided for the women, and drank three huge vessels of mead. Loki made haste to explain this prodigious appetite by saying that the bride had been fasting for eight days and nights in her longing for Jotunheim.

"After the banquet, Thrym, eager to kiss his bride, lifted the veil concealing Thor's features. The giant leaped back the length of the hall at sight of the fiery eyes of the war god. Loki was again quick to explain. For eight days and eight nights the bride had not slept, he explained, so great was her longing for Jotunheim.

"Finally, the giant's sister came, asking the customary bridal fee. Rings of gold were taken from the supposed bride's fingers to satisfy Thrym's sister. Then Thrym commanded the hammer to be brought; this he placed on the bride's knee while he invoked the blessing of Vor, goddess of vows. Thor immediately seized the hammer, killed the giant and his sister and all the guests, and made his way in triumph back to Asgard to celebrate his feat with weeks of gluttonous feasting and drinking."

"A proper home for giants and gods," declared Edvard, admiring a wild cataract plunging noisily down the face of a high cliff.

"Too eerie for me," admitted his father. "Too lonely. I like a landscape with farms and pastures and a few cherry trees."

It is doubtful if Edvard heard, for he was lost in admiration of the wild scene before him. Unlike his father, he liked best the rugged and the untamed landscapes. Amid such scenes he could get closest to the heart of his strange, melancholy land.

Night closed down upon them before they reached shelter. The stars seemed so bright and near that Edvard felt that he might reach his hand up and pluck them, as he would daisies in a springtime meadow.

"What do you know!" cried his father suddenly. "The Northern Lights! We shall have an early winter, that much is sure, when we see the lights at this season."

Faint luminous fingers were reaching over the jagged outline of the northern mountains. As Edvard and his father watched, the glow grew more pronounced, shoot-

ing out long streamers, fan-shaped, toward the zenith.
Faintly purple and blue at first, they changed to flame,
as if the sun had made a second setting, directly over the
magnetic pole. Edvard watched the display until his
father clucked to the horses and led the way down into
a valley where the lights of a little village winked
invitingly.

Next day they found themselves in the pleasant Valdres
region. Clear rushing streams and wide rolling farmlands
made a friendly landscape, and this was more to Edvard's
father's taste than the wild Jotunheim. Edvard, however, dreamed of the rugged heights and silent wastes,
and the sound of falling water lingered in his inner ear
for the whole of the journey.

Their way through Valdres led them past Fagernes and
the Randsfjord, then on south to Christiania, which lies
at the head of Oslofjord. They made a brief stay in the
bustling city, where Edvard Grieg was later to spend
eight hard years "among the dry-goods and railway interests." At Christiania they took ship for Denmark.

In Denmark they visited Edvard's cousin Nina and her
parents at the Kronborg Castle farm, near Helsingör.
Nina's father was Herman Hagerup, brother of Edvard's
mother. Nina's mother was a famous Danish actress, from
whom Nina had inherited a beautiful singing voice and
a remarkable dramatic talent. Edvard found this cousin
of his very charming indeed, quite as good company as
his sister Elisabeth at home, who was just Nina's age.

In Denmark, Edvard said goodbye to his father. He
was placed in the care of an old friend of the family, who

accompanied him across the North Sea to Hamburg. Many years later Edvard wrote about his arrival in Germany:

"I was sent under the care of an old friend of my father's. Over the North Sea we went to Hamburg, and after staying a day there, went on southward by train to mediæval Leipzig, whose dark, gloomy high houses and narrow streets fairly took my breath away. I was delivered at a pension. Father's old friend said goodbye, the last Norwegian words I heard for a long time, and there stood I, a fifteen-year-old boy, alone in that strange land among strange people. Homesickness seized me—I went into my room where I sat and cried without stopping till I was fetched for the midday meal by my hosts. The husband, a worthy Saxon Oberpostsecretär, tried to comfort me. 'See, my dear Herr Grieg, we have the same sun, the same moon, the same good God here that you have at home.' Very well meant. But neither sun nor moon nor der liebe Gott could make up for my father's friend, now receding from me, the last link binding me to home."

Die St. Thomas Kirche

Chapter Eight

And lusty lads roam here and there
So merrily
And ever among so merrily.

HENRY IV

A GOOD night's rest in the little room high under the attic roof of the good Oberpostsecretär's house and Edvard was himself again. His German hostess served him a hearty meal of coffee cakes, milk and cheese, and sausages somewhat like those that Ingrid made at Christmas time. She made jokes with him in German. Edvard, remembering the time he had brought his *Variations on a German Melody* to school instead of his German dictionary and grammar, felt for the first time that his stern teacher might have been right in punishing him. Some of his hostess' conversation was lost to him, and he puckered his forehead with the effort it cost him to get the

81

meaning of colloquial speech in a language not his own.

The Norwegian tongue is akin to German, however, and Edvard had not always neglected his German lessons, either. It was very soon that his language difficulties, like his first homesickness, were things of the past. Grieg wrote in later years:

"Soon I got over my homesickness and, though I hadn't a scrap of understanding of what it really meant to study music, I was perfectly sure the miracle would happen— that at the end of my three years of study I should come home again a wizard in the kingdom of sound! This is the best proof of my great naïveté, that it was the child in me that ruled completely. And I do not wish to be regarded as anything but a child conservatory student, since that is what I was, even to my clothes. I wore a short blouse belted at the waist, such as boys at home wore."

When Edvard went next day to the buildings which housed the Conservatory, he was assigned to classes by the kindly Director, Herr Conrad Schleinitz. "My fellow pupils looked me up and down at first," recorded Grieg in his memoir of his childhood. "There was indeed a violin player who amused himself by taking me on his knee, which reduced me to desperation. But all that was soon over."

Edvard had expected a miracle to happen—to gain a knowledge of music without effort. The miracle did not occur, and Edvard's first feeling was one of disappointment. He found that studying music, like studying anything else, was likely to be very tedious at times.

His first piano teacher was an unfortunate introduction

to the faculty. This teacher was Louis Plaidy. Grieg told in later years how dull Plaidy's method was. He would sit beside his pupil, listening to the playing; to hear better, he bent his right ear forward with his forefinger. All the while he kept up a monotonous chant of, "Slowly, strong, bring it out! Slowly, strong, bring it out!" until the student could hardly bear the sound any longer.

"Watch!" whispered one of the students to Edvard one day as they sat in Plaidy's class, waiting for the teacher to show how one of Mendelssohn's Fantasias should be played. Plaidy seated himself at the keyboard, played the slow introduction, but as soon as he came to the difficult, fast passages, he rose from his seat, turned to the class, and said, "And so forth."

"I don't think the old boy can play one piece clear through," declared Edvard's companion.

Edvard did not believe that exactly; for he knew that Louis Plaidy had been invited to the faculty of the Conservatory by Mendelssohn himself, and that many students learned from him successfully. But Edvard acknowledged to himself that he was merely bored by the teaching of Plaidy, and it was not until he began to study with Ernst Wenzel and Ignaz Moscheles that Edvard grew to love the study hours rather than to dread them.

Ernst Wenzel had been a fellow student and warm friend of Robert Schumann in the days when they both attended the old Leipzig University. Because he spoke English, most of the English-speaking students were in his class. These included five boys who were later to become musical leaders in their native England—Franklin Taylor and Walter Bacher, pianists; Edward Dannreuther, pianist and champion of Wagner in England; John Francis Barnett, famous teacher; and Arthur Seymour Sullivan of "Gilbert and Sullivan" fame.

Of Wenzel, Grieg once said: "He had a masterly way of imparting to me his interpretations; he could explain a bar in detail with far more penetration than Plaidy and, above all, there was music behind his words."

One of the boys from England—the Irish Arthur Sullivan—showed great promise at the Conservatory. Edvard Grieg admired the Irish boy's wit and his comprehensive knowledge of orchestral music, gained under the direction of the elder Sullivan in England. While he was still in Leipzig, Sullivan composed music as a setting for Shakespeare's *Tempest*. He wrote a few bars of this music in Grieg's album of autographs. This was the same Arthur Sullivan who was to win fame for his delightful comic operas like *The Mikado, The Pirates of Penzance, H.M.S. Pinafore,* and many others.

As a rule, Grieg and Sullivan met only on the grounds of the Conservatory and in classes there. Each had his own friends outside. Grieg was surprised, therefore, to hear his name called one evening as he was on his way to a Gewandhaus performance, and to see the smiling Arthur Sullivan hurrying up with a roll of manuscript under his arm.

"I say, Grieg! I have a real prize here! Herr Schleinitz has allowed me to take Mendelssohn's own manuscript of *St. Paul,* which is to be performed tonight. Should you like to follow it with me?"

Grieg knew that this manuscript was one of the prized possessions of the school, and wondered how the Irish lad had been able to persuade the Director of the Conservatory to let him take it.

"You must have a special gift of speech, Sullivan. Nobody else could have walked off with that score."

Sullivan laughed. "It's the Irish tongue. We all kiss the Blarney stone, you see." Locking his arm under one of Grieg's he drew him along to the old inner city, to the Drapers' Hall, which was the Gewandhaus of their day.

Concerts in the Gewandhaus, as both Sullivan and Grieg knew, represented the concerts of oldest standing in existence. They date from the time of Bach, when he was Cantor of Thomasschule. Under Mendelssohn, the concerts acquired world-wide fame in the years 1835 to 1843. Following Mendelssohn, Niels Gade, the great man of Scandinavian music, had conducted the brilliant Gewandhaus orchestra for four years before returning to his native Denmark.

For Grieg, the strangeness had long since worn off the gloomy city of Leipzig. He had grown to like the high-pitched roofs of the old houses and to find the narrow winding streets full of interest. Behind the market square was a labyrinth of crooked streets interconnected by covered courtyards and alleys. With the Danish boy, Emil Hornemann, and other friends from the Conservatory, Grieg often explored these quaint thoroughfares. Along these old streets and alleys were extensive warehouses and cellars, each with its history or legend. Grieg soon was familiar with all the old buildings with a story to tell—

the old Rathaus, a Gothic structure built in 1556; the Königshaus, for several centuries the palace of the Saxon kings in Leipzig; Paulinerkirche, built in the early thirteenth century; Thomaskirche, dating from 1496, famous mostly because the great Johann Sebastian Bach was organist there; the old University building, dating from 1409; Auerbach's *Hof,* built about 1530. Auerbach's was immortalized in Goethe's *Faust.* It was interesting in Grieg's day, as it is in this, for the curious old wine cellar with its mural paintings dating from the sixteenth century, representing the legend on which Goethe's play is based.

Ignaz Moscheles, friend of Beethoven and teacher of Mendelssohn, was another teacher whom Grieg found interesting and sympathetic. Grieg, in writing of those early "successes" so important to his later life, said:

"Hard things are said of old Moscheles as a teacher. I must defend him with the utmost warmth. It is true that he was naïve enough to believe that he could impress us when during lessons he set himself on all possible occasions to run down Chopin and Schumann, whom in secret I loved. But he could and did play beautifully, sometimes for almost the whole of the lesson. Specially fine were his renderings of Beethoven, whom he adored. They were faithful, full of character, and noble without any striving after effect. I studied with him dozens of Beethoven's sonatas. Often I had not played four bars before he would lay his hands over mine, push me gently off the stool and say, 'Now listen to what I make of it.' In this way I was initiated into many small technical secrets and learned to appreciate to the full his brilliant interpretations.

"It was said at the Conservatory—though as luck would have it I did not witness it myself—that during lessons he would give his pupils the following advice: 'Play diligently the old masters, Mozart, Beethoven, Haydn—and me.' I cannot vouch for the truth of this, but mention it because at his desire I grappled with his twenty-four Studies, Opus 70, which I do not regret having studied with him indefatigably from beginning to end. I liked them and did my best to satisfy both him and myself. He may have taken note of that, since he became steadily more sympathetic toward me. And a quite simple, to be sure, but for me momentous 'Success' it was when one day, after I had played one of his studies without having been stopped once, he turned to the other pupils and said, 'See, gentlemen, that is musical piano playing.' How happy I was! That day the whole world was bathed in sunshine for me."

Grieg studied harmony with E. F. Richter, author of the standard work on the subject, and with Dr. Robert Pappernitz. Grieg's Norwegianism was already beginning to assert itself at this time, and he found himself constantly at odds with the teachers of harmony, particularly with Richter, who insisted upon his pupils' adhering to strict rules and never asking "Why?" Already Grieg was seeking new harmonic combinations, experimenting with the chromatic scale, fretting at the bonds which strict classical form imposed upon him.

Moritz Hauptmann was a teacher more to Grieg's taste. Grieg's own vivid words give a picture of this grand old man of music:

"Finally I had lessons from Moritz Hauptmann, and I still thank that dear old man for all he taught me through his fine and intelligent observations. In spite of all his learning, he represented for me the absolute anti-scholastic. For him rules signified nothing in themselves but were an expression of nature's laws. An episode that in a weak moment I might call a 'success,' I will put in here. Before I knew Hauptmann—I was not yet sixteen and still wore my child's blouse—I had attained in Privat-Prüfung (a kind of yearly examination in which all the pupils, without exception, had to take part) the honor of being allowed to play a piano piece of my own composition. When I had finished and had left the piano, I saw to my great surprise an elderly gentleman get up from the teacher's table and come towards me. He laid his hand on my shoulder and said only, 'Good day, my boy. We must be good friends.' It was Hauptmann. Naturally I loved him from that moment. Ill as he was in the last years of his life, he gave lessons at his home, the Thomasschule, Sebastian Bach's old residence. Here I had the happiness of getting to know him more intimately. I remember him on his sofa in dressing gown and slippers, his spectacles almost touching my book of studies, which still retains more than one spot of the yellow brown snuff that was always dripping from his snuffy nose. He used to sit with a big handkerchief in his hand so as to forestall the drops. But he had no luck. Then it was used as a cloth to wipe the book of studies, where its traces are still plain to see."

In later years Grieg often complained that the instruction at Leipzig was inadequate. He bitterly blamed the school for the fact that he was given no instruction in violin-playing, and for the haphazard way he was introduced to the rules of orchestration.

Chapter Nine

Youth like summer morn, age like winter weather.
THE PASSIONATE PILGRIM

GRIEG'S last years at the Conservatory were a sort of under-the-surface struggle with the dictates of teachers who would not accept the newer trends in musical composition. Chopin and Schumann were frowned upon by the faculty. Wagner was considered positively disreputable.

In 1861, Carl Reinecke was appointed conductor of the Gewandhaus concerts and master at the Conservatory. Reinecke clung to the old classical forms of music. Students like Grieg, who were reaching out toward a new form of expression, he merely regarded with a lofty sort of pity. Though he did not forbid the experiments with harmony which were absorbing Grieg more and more, he greeted them with indifference. His guidance of such students was lax to the point of neglect.

Grieg described Reinecke's method—or lack of it—as teacher of composition: "To illustrate how things went at those lessons, I will only say that I who had announced that I knew nothing whatever of either the theory of form or the technique of string instruments was ordered to write a string quartet. I felt that a thing like that might as well have been proposed to me by our porter N. N.— so utterly absurd I thought it. It made me think of my old nurse. If she wanted me to do something I didn't feel able to and objected, 'I can't,' she would answer. 'Put *can't* away from you and take hold with both hands.' This saying, which has many a time put courage in me, did it here too. What Reinecke did not teach me I tried to pick up for myself from Mozart and Beethoven, whose quartets I studied diligently on my own initiative. I got through my task in some kind of way, the parts were written out and were played by my fellow students at one of our private ensembles. The director of the Conservatory was in favor of the performance of the quartet at a Haupt-Prüfung (public performance of the best work of the students). But Ferdinand David, the distinguished violinist and teacher, who was present at the rehearsal, thought otherwise. He took me aside and gave me the advice—as well meant as it was wise—not to let the quartet be performed."

Ferdinand David explained: "The public will not take kindly to this music. They will call it *the music of the future*." That was exactly what the public, particularly the German public, did call Grieg's music for many years, but eventually the world caught up with the creator of the "harmony of the future." It was a German critic who at last admitted that "Grieg has added a new string to our lyre."

After the string quartet Reinecke decided that his pupil should write an overture. Grieg was aghast.

"I, who hadn't a notion either of orchestral instruments or of orchestration, was to write an overture! Again I thought of our porter, N. N., and of ——, my nurse. I set to work with the reckless abandonment of youth. But this time I was defeated. I sat literally stuck fast in the middle of the overture and could not get any further.

"It was fortunate for me that I heard so much fine music in Leipzig, especially orchestral and chamber music. That compensated for the instruction in the technique of composition which I did *not* get at the Conservatory. It developed my mind and my musical critical sense to the highest degree, but at the same time it confused the relationship between what I wanted to do and what I was capable of doing, and this confusion was the result of my stay in Leipzig. It would have seemed to me quite natural if neither the director of the Conservatory nor the teachers had taken any interest in me, for in the three or four years I was there I achieved nothing that could awaken expectations of a future. When, therefore, in these glimpses of the Conservatory I have had to find fault with several things, both in persons and in the institution, I hasten to add that I take it for granted that it was, first and foremost, my own nature that led to my going out of the Conservatory almost as ignorant as when I went in. I was a dreamer with no turn for competition. I was heavy, not very communicative, and anything but quick to learn. We Norwegians develop, as a rule, too slowly to be able to show fully at eighteen what we are capable of. However that may be, I didn't in the least know how to deal with myself."

There is no doubt that Grieg was much too hard on himself when he declared that he had learned nothing at Leipzig and that the teachers found him unpromising. The certificate given him upon his graduation in 1862 indicated that Edvard Grieg was graduated from the Conservatory with highest honors. It is typical of Grieg, whose modesty concerning his work amounted almost to pessimism at times, that he put this certificate away and said no more about it. Not until many years after his death was it found among some old papers and published in a musical paper.

Besides the testimony of the certificate, there is the evidence of his two collections of piano pieces and songs, composed during his student years at Leipzig. These were published as Opus 1 and Opus 2.

Opus 1 consists of four pieces for piano, dedicated to Grieg's teacher Wenzel. These were the pieces which the young composer played at the public performance in the Gewandhaus at Easter time in 1862, just before his graduation. The first three bars of No. 1 of this opus* show the extreme simplicity of the young composer's first attempt to put his musical thought on paper, though it has originality. In the other tone poems of this collection, we

* See Appendix, page 243.

see the growth of the young composer in sureness of
form, in harmonic elaboration, in the rich and comprehensive use of the instrument. Toward the end of the
fourth piece there is a shrill dissonance, a form of expression which was to become a characteristic of Grieg's
music.

In the four songs for contralto, Opus 2, there is strong
evidence of the influence of the German Romantics—
Weber, Schubert, Schumann, Mendelssohn. However,
there is evidence also of a vital, original artist, searching
for his own expression. Grieg's later magnificent ability
to transform nature impressions into strange and beautiful
melodies and harmonies begins to show up in this work.
One of the songs, written to a poem of the great Heinrich
Heine, begins, "I am encompassed by gray clouds." A
feeling for nature in its grotesque and somber moods is
conjured up richly in this song, and its intensity of emotion gives a glimpse of great talent, sleeping, perhaps,
like Brünnhilde on her fire-girt rock, but on the verge
of waking.

During the Leipzig days two events occurred which
were to have a tremendous influence on the future course
of Grieg's life. One was a near-tragic piece of ill luck.
In the early spring of 1860 young Edvard Grieg, who had
learned the lesson that hard work and not dreaming was
to accomplish the miracle of making him a great musician
and composer, broke down under the heavy tasks which
he had set himself. He had a severe attack of pleurisy, and
was so ill that his mother came from Norway to Leipzig
to nurse him.

When he was well enough to travel, she took him home to Landås. There a summer of rest and quiet pleasures restored him to health—not quite to full health, though, for the pleurisy had destroyed one of his lungs. Ever afterward, one of his shoulders was a little higher than the other and one side of his chest depressed. Edvard, never very robust, was to have the burden of increasingly poor health to bear all his life. This fact alone accounts for the fact that he composed only in the shorter forms— piano pieces, songs, a few sonatas—and produced no symphony or opera, though such works as his great Piano Concerto and the *Olaf Trygvason* music showed him capable of fine work in the longer forms.

The other event of great importance was the hearing of Wagner's *Tannhäuser*. Though this work did not represent the later Wagner, it was an important and revolutionary opera. Its music, frowned upon by the older musicians, was catching the ear of the youngsters. Grieg was among the young moderns. "By 1858 *Tannhäuser* had appeared," he wrote, "and it impressed me so much that I heard it fourteen times running."

Discarding the old ideas of operatic writing, according to which the libretto often consisted of disconnected scenes, and the music of arias and duets was inserted without much regard for the action or plot, Wagner wrote his operas so that there was continuity, with music descriptive of the mood of the poem to create a harmony of ideas and emotion. His later music was to carry this idea still further in the *leitmotif*—that is, a few bars of music descriptive of each character of the story, introduced into the score at appropriate points. This close association of music and words, this use of music to infuse the thought of a poem with feeling, appealed strongly to Grieg. This same welding of idea and sound was to be Grieg's characteristic in the 150 songs he wrote.

How young Grieg must have thrilled to the wild bacchante rhythms of the dancers in the Hill of Venus in the opening scene! And in scene three, the haunting melody of the young shepherd's song to Dame Holda, goddess of spring and flocks, must have made the young Norwegian lad not a little homesick for the valleys and fjords of his home, where lonely shepherds in high upland pastures made plaintive music on *lur* and *landleike,* ancient horn and harp of Norway.

> "Dame Holda stepped from the mountain's heart
>   To roam thro' wood and thro' meadow;
> Sweet sound and low around me did start—
>   I longed I might follow her shadow.
> And there dreamt I a golden dream,
> And when again the day did gleam,
> The spell was gone that bound me:
> 'Twas May, sweet May, around me.
>   New songs of joy attune my lay,
>   For May hath come—the balmy May!"

With what youthful sympathy Edvard must have followed the sorrows of Elisabeth and listened to her prayer to the Virgin:

> "Oh, blessed Virgin, hear my prayer!
> Thou star of glory, look on me!

Here in the dust I bend before thee,
Now from this earth, oh set me free.
Now from this earth, oh set me free!"

How faithful Wolfram, mourning for Elisabeth, and the minstrel Tannhäuser, singing his own sorrow to the evening star, must have won Grieg's heart! And one can be sure that the young Norwegian returned to his student's room with the yearning melody of the song to the evening star sounding over and over in his inner ear:

"O thou sublime, sweet evening star,
Joyful I greet thee from afar!"

And the exultant phrases of the Chorus of Pilgrims must have given the sensitive youth no peace for many a day after its majestic harmonies were stilled.

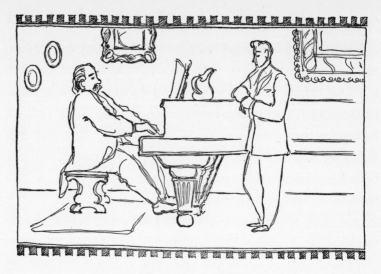

Chapter Ten

But when I came to man's estate,
With hey, ho, the wind and the rain.

TWELFTH NIGHT

GRIEG left the Leipzig Conservatory in the spring of 1862, before his eighteenth birthday. In May he was at home in Bergen, preparing to give his first independent concert. This event took place in the great hall of the Workers' Society in the latter part of May. The hometown newspaper *Bergenposten* gave Grieg's performance unqualified praise next day:

"The high reputation which had preceded him does not seem to have been exaggerated. His compositions were singularly pleasing and it would seem that Herr Grieg has a great future before him as a composer. As an executant also he won universal applause, especially in the Schumann quartet for piano and strings which might be called the crowning feature of the concert."

Following his success with his first concert in Bergen, Grieg came face to face with reality. How was he to make a living? His father, who had sent John to Leipzig for a time to study 'cello and had spent a considerable sum on Edvard's four years at the Conservatory, felt that his youngest son must henceforth support himself without help from home. Apparently the best way to make a start toward an independent life was to apply for one of the Norwegian government grants to persons of talent to permit them to travel and study.

"The thing to do is to write the Royal Ecclesiastical and Educational Department," declared Edvard's mother.

Much thought and discussion went into the preparation of the important application. Anxious days of waiting followed the sending of the letter. When the answer came, it brought gloomy disappointment for young Grieg: there was to be no stipend for the young student of nineteen.

"Never mind," comforted Grieg's mother. "We shall find a way. Take the money you made from the concert and buy orchestral scores. You say you need more knowledge of orchestral composition. Very well, then stay at home with us this winter and get this knowledge. Energy is the main thing, Edvard!"

"And I shall work though my back breaks," laughed Edvard, imitating his mother's favorite declaration.

Mother Grieg had to laugh with her son, but she shook a warning finger at him nevertheless. "Hard work and no dreaming—that must be your order of the day," she warned him.

Father Grieg fell in with their plans: for truth to tell,

he was as pleased as the rest of the family to have his talented son at home again. Edvard's mother cleared out a storehouse at the back of the main dwelling of Landås. When this storeroom had been furnished with desk and piano and small stove, Edvard Grieg had his first studio, where he could work quietly and undisturbed.

It was an eccentricity of Grieg's—one which he shared with Beethoven and several other great composers—that he could not work when people listened to him. He was extremely sensitive to criticism, and it was this sensitiveness to being overheard, rather than an aversion to noise and confusion, which made it impossible for him to work either at home or in hotel rooms—in any place, in fact, where people were paying attention to him. In later years, he did all his best work in isolated work huts, such as the famous "piano-box" houses he built at Lofthus and at his home of Troldhaugen.

Edvard worked diligently that winter at Landås. He set himself the task of acquiring a systematic knowledge of orchestration and the principles of musical form which he had not mastered at Leipzig. When spring came round again and the blossoms hung like snow on the apple trees, he had mastered most of the technical difficulties of orchestral composition.

A great restlessness seized him. What was he to do to make a start in the world? Obviously, he could not remain at home forever, studying in his little workroom. As for composing, the year at Bergen had brought forth very little. He had written a work for choir and piano— *Rückblick*—and this was all. After the performance of this work by the Harmonic Society on April 27, 1863, Grieg sighed unhappily.

"Not very much to show for a year's work," he said when his father and mother congratulated him.

"Patience, Edvard, patience," his mother told him. "You will find a way, I know."

The urge to get away from Bergen became ever stronger. This time it was not Leipzig that called, but Copenhagen in Denmark. In Copenhagen the great Niels Gade lived, and Johann Hartman, noted Danish composer. Emil Hartmann, son of Johann, was also in Denmark, become a great composer under the tutorship of his father and of his brother-in-law, Niels Gade. These were the great men of Scandinavia, as far as music was concerned. A sure instinct was turning Grieg away from the German Romantics toward a northern spirit in music. This voice of the North, melancholy and tender, had been introduced into music for the first time by the elder Hartmann. Gade's early genius—somewhat blurred, it is true, by his years at Leipzig—had found inspiration in the northern sources. All these men represented a spirit in music which was more congenial to Grieg than the Classic-Romantic tradition of Leipzig.

"I was simply wrecked after my stay in Leipzig," Grieg once wrote in a letter to Iver Holter, musician friend from Christiania. "I did not know which way to turn when an indefinable longing drove me toward Copenhagen."

Grieg received a small loan from his father, and in May he went to Copenhagen. There he sought out Gade, whose northern imagination Mendelssohn had once described as "kindling the Northern Lights."

Grieg called at Gade's home with a feeling of great inward excitement. He was looking for direction for the turn his musical composition should take. He was like a traveler, lost and inquiring his way, unable to give the name of his destination, having only a vague idea of the kind of place it was, and no idea at all of where it lay. Aimless and bewildered, he was not unlike the youth in the old story his nurse had told him many times—the youth who sought his lost love in a land that he knew only as being "East o' the sun and West o' the moon."

Gade received Grieg rather coldly. His first question was, "Have you written anything?"

"Nothing of importance," was Grieg's modest answer. His schoolboy pieces seemed hardly worth mentioning to the stern, assured composer with whom he was speaking.

"Then go home and write a symphony," was all that Gade had to say.

Feeling not a little cast down by this meeting with Gade, Grieg made his way back to his rooms. He sat at his desk for a long time, brooding and unhappy. Then the words of his old nurse came to his aid again.

"Put *can't* away from you and take hold with both hands!"

In an almost angry mood, Grieg set to work. In two weeks' time he had completed the first movement of a symphony, fully orchestrated.

With his work rolled under his arm, he sought out Gade again. As he walked to the great man's studio, his

thoughts were less embittered than they had been for
some time. He could take pleasure again in looking at the
beech trees along the streets of the pleasant Danish city,
where the storks nested in every quaint chimney pot. Birds
returning with the spring made an excited chatter under
the eaves of an ivy-covered church.

"Well, I see you have the symphony!" Gade was in
good mood. He sat down immediately at his grand piano
to try the composition. The music was fresh and charming. In one place a little passage built up plaintively on
the chromatic scale gave a hint of the later Grieg.

It was said that when Gade was pleased with a piece of
music, he invariably drank great quantities of water as he
played. This day he emptied a large pitcher. At the end
of the interview, he patted the young composer on the
back in a genial way and said heartily, "Continue your
excellent symphony, Herr Grieg. It is sound work."

Though Grieg was pleased with Gade's words, he
knew that the music was more a product of Leipzig than
of the new trend he was seeking. He lost interest in the
symphony. It took him a year to write the remaining
parts, and he never allowed the work to be published. In
later years, he arranged the *adagio* and the *intermezzo* as
a piano duet; this version was published as Opus 14.

Grieg turned from the older Gade to younger musical
friends: Emil Hornemann, Edvard's school chum at Leipzig, the young composers August Winding and Gottfred
Matthison-Hansen, the singer Julius Stenberg, and the
writer Benjamin Feddersen—all of whom remained his
staunch friends throughout his life.

With these young men he dined and roamed the country lanes, went to concerts and operas, organized amateur theatricals, played his own compositions and listened to theirs. The result of Grieg's association with these northern artists was the composition of six piano pieces—*Six Poetic Tone Pictures,* Opus 3, and *Six Songs,* Opus 4.

In the *Six Poetic Tone Pictures* Grieg is already moving toward the North, especially in No. 1 and No. 5. No. 2 shows the influence of Schumann. There is something of Chopin in No. 4. No. 6 is reminiscent of Mendelssohn's *Midsummer Night's Dream* music. The first four bars of No. 3* are enough to show that Grieg was already casting his musical thoughts in harmonies bold and novel.

In the *Six Songs,* Opus 4, to poems of Heine, Chamisso, and Uhland, Grieg makes use of the old Greek modes or scales. These old scales had been used in the church until the early sixteenth century, and are still to be heard when the Gregorian chants are performed.

The Greek modes differ from our modern scales (major, melodic minor and harmonic minor, and chromatic) in the same way that these scales differ from one another— that is, in the spacing of intervals. The oldest mode was called the Aeolian mode, its intervals being the same as those of the white notes of the piano between A and A. The mode by which all the ancient Greek lyres were tuned was the Dorian mode; the intervals of this mode, whatever the pitch, are those of the white keys of the piano between one D and the next.

* See Appendix, page 243.

These ancient modes were used in the native Norwegian music. Though Norse music had not been played in Grieg's childhood home, and though he had not yet come in contact with the rich sources of folk music in his country, in his *Six Songs* he used as if by instinct the ancient modes to give an antique tone to his music.

"There was an old king" from Opus 4* has features from the Aeolian mode to give the music a feeling of old and far-off times. The musical setting for Heine's words expresses the ballad tone of the poem:

> "There was a king of old time:
> His heart was heavy, gray his head;"

And for the ill-fated sweethearts, the music yearns tenderly:

> " 'Tis sweet of sound, yet full of woe,
> How both were doomed to perish, they loved one
> another so."

It was about this time that Grieg made his first acquaintance with Danish poetry. He set five of the poems of Christian Winther to music. The poetry is simple and direct; Grieg with unerring instinct for the proper mood made his musical setting simple also. They stand close to folk song in innocence and grace. Four songs—"Thanksgiving," "Forest Song," "The Flowers Speak," and "Song on the Mountains"—make up this collection, published years later as Opus 10.

One other friend of the Denmark days must be mentioned. Grieg first saw him after a concert in Copenhagen

* See Appendix, page 243.

—a tall, awkward man with a compelling smile and the largest feet in the whole of Scandinavia, Edvard felt sure.

"Who is that?" Grieg wanted to know.

"Andersen. Hans Christian Andersen. You know—the one who writes plays and poems and the fairy tales," explained a friend. "Want to meet him?"

That is how Grieg came to know the genial poet of Denmark, the man who never quite grew up. Loving and understanding children, he made all the children of the world a unique present—a collection of fairy tales full of humor and pathos and charm. The author of "The Elder-Tree Mother," "The Little Match Girl," "The Fir Tree," "The Tin Soldier," and many other tales held out his hand to musical young Grieg and smiled his warm smile as he said, "We must get to know each other better; I have heard of your great talent."

Grieg and Andersen grew to be warm friends. The Danish poet was among the first to appreciate what Grieg was looking for in the North—the folk spirit in music. To words of Andersen's Grieg wrote, in all, eighteen songs, four of these composed in the winter of 1864 and published as Opus 5 under the title *Melodies of the Heart*. This was the first work to make Grieg's name known in Scandinavian countries.

All of the songs of Opus 5, dedicated to "Hr. Professor H. C. Andersen with admiration and esteem," bear the mark of the smiling, graceful Denmark scenery, which is a striking contrast to the rugged Norwegian landscape. No. 3 of the collection, the famous "I Love Thee," has been called the greatest love song ever written.

There is a story behind the beautiful love lyric called simply "I Love Thee." The song is a confession of Grieg's own emotions at this time. He had fallen in love, and the girl of his choice was his cousin Nina Hagerup, she of the beautiful voice and entrancingly feminine ways.

Grieg had carried with him to Leipzig the memory of his bright-eyed cousin, whom he had visited on his way to the Conservatory. She was one of the first persons he had called on when he came from Bergen in 1863. At her home, crowds of young people met to sing and play, and Nina always delighted them with her clear voice and deep understanding of music. She, like Edvard, was an artist of distinction, though she did not make use of her talents outside her home.

These two young people, short and blonde and quaint as two elves from Norway, were drawn more and more together. In July 1864 (Nina related in years to come), "We played Schumann's B flat major symphony as a duet —and got engaged."

When Nina's parents were asked for their consent, they flew into a rage. Fru Hagerup particularly opposed the match. Her first husband had been an artist, and she knew from experience the insecurity of the artistic life. Bitterly Fru Hagerup protested to all her friends: "This Edvard Grieg he *is* nobody, he *has* nothing, and nobody listens to his music!"

It is related that after his betrothal to Nina, Grieg was never in his father-in-law's home, and that Edvard and Nina had to arrange their meetings in secret, on the streets of Copenhagen or in the woods outside of town.

In a mood of both breathless adventure and tender melancholy Grieg composed "I Love Thee" * for Nina:

"My thought of thoughts, my very inmost being,
Thou only art my heart's felicity!
I love thee more than all else under heaven,
I love but thee, I love but thee,
I love but thee thro' all eternity!
I love but thee thro' all eternity!"

* See Appendix, page 244.

Chapter Eleven

Tell me where is fancy bred,
Or in the heart or in the head?
How begot, how nourishèd?
Reply, reply.

THE MERCHANT OF VENICE

$\mathcal{I}$N THE summer of 1864 Grieg returned to Norway. At Landås his little workroom was put in order, but something was lacking to stimulate the young composer to creative activity. He was just twenty-one, eager to make his mark in the world, secure at last in his knowledge of the difficult musical forms. His whole creative nature was seething and burning within him; yet he could not find a way to express himself. Restlessness and discontent possessed him once more.

When discontent and self-doubt were on the point of making him wretched, Ole Bull came to the rescue. It was a middle-aged Ole Bull with whom Grieg renewed his acquaintance that summer—a man of fifty-four, who had made a complete success of his career. Returning from exhausting concert tours of Europe and America, Ole Bull had bought the beautiful country house of Valestrand, on the Island of Osteröen, which was twenty miles north and east of Bergen.

"Come over to Valestrand," was an often-renewed invitation for Grieg. Whenever the hopelessness of forcing his imagination to take form in musical composition made the young composer melancholy, he closed his piano, locked his study, and took one of the little steamers to Osteröen. Sometimes the trip took two hours, sometimes four; it all depended on the number of lighters loaded with wood or farm produce which the steamer stopped to draw from one wharf to the next.

One August day Edvard and his brother came out to Osteröen together, John with his 'cello. Whenever business permitted, Edvard's talented elder brother joined Edvard and Ole Bull and the three musicians played trios together.

"This is just the sort of place one would imagine Ole Bull choosing for a home," said Edvard as the boat approached the harbor of Valestrand, a tiny amphitheater of shallow water which permitted no large craft to dock. Only the little coastwise steamers could tie up at the old moss-grown wharf. Bull's home overlooked the harbor and the village that nestled in the shelter of the protecting hills.

Though the house looked to be close to the water, it was

in reality a half-hour's walk from the dock. A pathway led past a boathouse with thatched roof out of which grew plumed grasses and a small birch tree. Stepping along on the mossy stones of this path, Edvard and his brother came to the one road of the island. Peasants from the village of Osteröen were making hay in the fields on either side of the road, and larks rose singing from the sweet grass straight in the face of the sun. Edvard made a mental note of the scene made vivid by the red jackets and embroidered blouses of the women. Wild pansies grew in cool shaded spots, and white clover and dandelions sprinkled the meadows, like a white and gold design on a green coverlet. These impressions of the Norwegian countryside would be transformed into musical sound in days not far off.

"There is Valestrand!" cried John.

The sight which met their eyes was enough to justify John's excitement. Low rolling hills swept back from the road to permit a view of the old farmhouse. The heather was in bloom on the lower hills, and the higher slopes were clothed with birch and fir. Valestrand stood high above the pink blooms of the heather like some fairy-tale palace.

It was a wooden house, painted a pale flesh color, with fantastic curving staircase leading to the front door. Oriental arches and a dome-crowned tower, somewhat like the dome of a Russian church, were droll additions to the typically Norwegian farmhouse; yet on this island of Osteröen they seemed less grotesque than they would have elsewhere. It was as if some special magic of the island demanded outlandish architecture and odd and fanciful human beings.

Ole Bull was odd enough and fanciful enough, in all conscience. He waved to John and Edvard from the high front veranda at the head of the curved stairs. A tall man in a swallow-tail coat, with a lock of bright hair falling near his right eye, he stood straight as a pine. His eyes lighted with pleasure as his guests came up the rose-bordered walk.

"Welcome to Valestrand!" he called. "Welcome, thrice welcome," he repeated in his fanciful way. And like a child displaying a treasure, he pointed to the clumps of wild pansies set all along the steps to the veranda. "In your honor. In your honor," he repeated, beaming happily when the two Griegs expressed their pleasure.

They had the midday meal—the Norwegian *middag*—with Ole Bull, his brisk little French wife, and his son Alexander. A maid in wide-winged headdress and scarlet jacket served them with trout, freshly caught, salad, strawberries, goat's-milk cheese, and fragrant gooseberry wine.

After the meal, the three musicians went into Ole Bull's study. It was a superb music-room, finished in yellow pine, with rows of twisted carved pillars, and carved cornices, beams, and panels.

"All made by Norwegian workmen," Bull said, pointing with pride to the polished woodwork and intricate carving.

"Somewhat different from my workroom at Landås," laughed Edvard.

"It isn't the workroom that turns out the work," Bull reminded him.

Edvard and Ole Bull first played a Mozart sonata, while John looked on, admiring the skillful technique of Bull's bowing and the grace of his brother's left hand. Like Mozart himself, Grieg was always noted for the great ease of his left-hand playing.

The great violinist was playing the favorite violin of his expensive collection. It was a creation of Gasparo da Salò, and for 150 years it had been in a museum at Innsbruck, in Austria. In 1809 French soldiers sacked the town and one of them carried off the famous old instrument. Later it was sold to Herr Rhehazek, a Viennese official who was a collector of violins. Ole Bull visited Vienna in 1839, saw the violin, and wanted to buy it; but Rhehazek would not sell his prized possession. He told Bull, however, that if the violin ever were put up for sale Bull would be informed. In 1841, while Bull was dining with Liszt and Mendelssohn in Leipzig, a letter was handed to him. It came from Rhehazek's son. Rhehazek was dead, and his son was faithfully carrying out his father's promise made to Bull two years before. The violin is now in the museum at Bergen, Norway.

When the sonata was at an end, John joined the violinist and pianist. For the rest of the long afternoon the great paneled study hummed and throbbed with music from the masters—Mozart, Beethoven, Weber, Mendelssohn, and many another composer loved by all three of them.

Though Ole Bull played the works of the old masters with great skill, he did not invest them with the same weird, unearthly quality which made his playing of Norway's native fiddle music an experience no listener ever forgot. The great Gasparo da Salò violin was at its best when it vibrated to the folk dances and songs of Möllargutten and the other fiddlers of Norwegian valleys and fjords. Ole Bull, in fact, was proud to be known as a folk musician—king of the *hardingfele* fiddlers—and his own compositions might well have been folk songs as old as Norway's mountains.

When the trio-playing was done, Edvard cried out, "Now we must have *Saeterjentens Sondag* [*Saeter Eirl's Sunday*]!"

Ole Bull smiled and drew his bow across the strings. The quiet, subdued music of the greatest of Bull's own compositions conjured up for his listeners the thin tinkling of cowbells and the faraway ringing of church bells. In the high mountain pasture the saeter-girl was spending her lonely Sunday, watching her flocks and herds, listening wistfully to the distant sound of the bells in the valley below.

At dinner that evening, there was a lively discussion of modern composers. Edvard spoke warmly of Wagner. Bull merely snorted. "Wagner ought to be lodged in a house of correction," he declared. "However, if you like his music," he added tolerantly, twinkling at Edvard, "I suppose the man is not entirely mad."

Many such days brightened that summer in Bergen.

Edvard and Ole Bull became close friends, wandering the hills near Bergen together, making short trips into the mountain regions to the north. These excursions were invaluable in shaping the course of Grieg's genius. Though he had no premonition of the fact, the nature impressions he was gathering were to burst forth brilliantly in the form of music when the right spark touched off the genius smoldering within him.

The trips with Bull took Edvard to grand, flower-carpeted valleys, where whispering winds made a melancholy soughing in the groves. They climbed the slopes of snow-crested mountains from which the midsummer's sun never departed. They tramped along brooks and streams and thundering rivers. By boat they went into the deep fjords and amongst the thousands of coastal islands.

The appearance of hundreds of rosy-cheeked peasant girls at the market square on *flyttledag* (moving day) was a sure sign that summer was over and the long winter about to begin. *Flyttledag* was the day in fall when all the servant girls in search of employment came in carts piled high with gaily painted hope chests and bundles to interview persons in the city. Among the goats, chickens, eggs, goat's-milk cheeses, and woolen goods of the marketplace, maids and housewives made their agreements for the year to come. Just about this time Edvard packed his own belongings, told his family goodbye, and set out once more for Denmark.

Nina was waiting eagerly for him, you may be sure. So were his good friends, Feddersen and Stenberg and Andersen and the rest. One of the great events of his life awaited him, too, but of this he had no notion at that time. This event was his meeting with Rikard Nordraak.

Some years later Grieg wrote of that meeting, which was to bear rich fruit: "What actually happened at my first meeting with Nordraak was so characteristic—of Nordraak—that I can conjure it up at will as if it were yesterday. It was one evening at Copenhagen's Tivoli that I was introduced by Fru Thoresen to a young man who called himself Nordraak and whose opening words were: 'And so we two great men really meet!' Bearing, gestures, voice, all suggested that here I had a man who felt himself the future Björnson plus Ole Bull. But there was, at the same time, something so touchingly naïve and lovable about him that he took me by storm. I had never, till that moment, considered the possibility of being or becoming a great man. I was a student, nothing more—timid, shy, and delicate. But this assurance of success was just the medicine for me, and from that moment it was as if we had been friends all our lives."

There was a certain humor in that meeting, for the "two great men" were very young—Grieg being twenty-one, and Nordraak twenty-two at the time. But, as Grieg himself realized, the meeting was a fateful one for him. Nordraak was able to point the way for Grieg's genius; he put an end for all time to the uneasy searching for expression which had made Grieg unhappy and insecure.

Nordraak, like Grieg, was Norwegian. His cousin was the writer Björnstjerne Björnson, some of whose poems Nordraak had set to music. These compositions included *Mary Stuart,* a scene from *Sigurd Slembe,* and many airs inspired by Björnson's peasant stories. He had also composed the beautiful national song, "Yes, we love the land that towers."

After their meeting at the Tivoli, Nordraak took Grieg home with him. Sitting down at the piano, the gay, red-haired Nordraak played his own compositions for Grieg, telling him that a Norwegian composer should turn to his people's folk songs, and to the familiar scenes of his native land for inspiration. The young visionary, whose chief genius lay in his ability to convey his enthusiasm to others, opened young Grieg's eyes to the value of the Norse folk music.

Writing of this brilliant Rikard Nordraak, Björnson, his cousin, once said: "He was all clarity and strength, a full round sum of Norwegian melodies and Norwegian national enthusiasm, Norwegian character sketches and anecdotes, Norwegian dreams and fairy stories, a profusion of plans for Norwegian operas and symphonies."

Nordraak was a person of great charm. Björnson told of his "red hair and freckles and . . . exceptionally delightful smile at once tender and merry. His good nature, humor, buoyancy, his playing, his compositions, his plans and his love affairs enveloped one like an unending springtime."

Such was the young man who fanned Grieg's genius to a white heat, so that in the space of a spring and summer Grieg mastered the exacting form of the sonata, made use of the ballad form, wrote two fine songs—*Autumn Storm* and *Outward Bound*—in addition to composing his first tone poems for piano, the *Humoresques,*

Opus 6—a form in which he was to do great work.

"I was longing," said Grieg, "to find expression for the best that was in me—a best that lay a thousand miles from Leipzig and its atmosphere; but that it lay in love of my fatherland and in my feeling for the great, melancholy Westland nature I did not know and would never perhaps have found out if I had not, through Nordraak, been led to self-examination. This had its first result in the Humoresques, Opus 6, dedicated to Nordraak, in which the direction of development is plainly shown. I willingly allow that Nordraak's influence was not entirely musical. But that is exactly what I am grateful to him for, that he opened my eyes to the importance of that in music which is *not* music."

Grieg was not familiar with the rich treasurehouse of Norse folk melody when he wrote the *Humoresques*. But on the walks with Grandfather Hagerup along the Tyskebrygge he had heard the Norwegian sailors and fisherfolk singing. At Trondhjem he had heard the peasant songs and the shepherd's pipe and the *lur*. In the Jotunheim he had heard the *hardingfele*. These impressions of Norse folk music he had absorbed through the skin, so to speak. The Norse color is certainly present in the *Humoresques*. A few bars of the delightful *menuetto** is enough to show us that Grieg was moving consciously at last to the expression of Norwegian nationalism in his music.

In the winter of 1864-65, Grieg and Nordraak founded a musical society at Copenhagen—the Euterpe—for the

* See Appendix, page 244.

fostering of interest in Norse art. The composer Horne-mann and the organist-composer Matthison-Hansen added their whole-hearted support to the Euterpe concerts, the object of which was the performance of Scandinavian works. Nordraak, naturally, conducted the first concert, which went very well, he wrote Björnson, though "the choir was scraped together in a terrific hurry and there was a great shortage of tenors." At the next Euterpe concert Grieg made his first appearance as conductor. The Adagio and Intermezzo from his symphony written at Gade's suggestion were produced for the first time at this concert.

In the spring of 1865 Nordraak went to Berlin. Grieg moved out to the village of Rungsted, where he spent the summer with the Danish author Benjamin Feddersen. There it was that the stimulus which Nordraak had given his genius began to take form. In eleven days he composed the Piano Sonata in E minor, Opus 7. The first movement of this sonata shows that Grieg knew how to write in strict form; he had forever mastered the technical difficulties. The music is gay and full of self-confidence. The Andante opens in gentle pastoral mood.* This quiet music, graceful and melodious, is very soon interrupted by fortissimo outbursts. The effect is as if a traveler, walking along a flower-carpeted valley, came suddenly upon a rushing river. There is an Intermezzo, as quiet as a peaceful scene in rural Norway, and suddenly the quiet is broken by a lively dance—the fiddlers, perhaps, on St. John's Eve. Then, as suddenly as it began, the dancing

* See Appendix, page 245.

breaks off, and we are again in the pastoral scene called up by the main theme. The Minuet is entirely Teutonic music, vigorous, strong, with broad chords. The finale is wild, tempestuous music, like a sudden storm over the mountains. The coda, built upon the second subject of the finale, ends triumphantly and joyously.

Grieg followed his piano sonata with his first Violin Sonata, in F major, Opus 8. The ideas, so long dammed up, were released and swept forth in a veritable flood. One charming fancy follows another, mood follows mood in a wealth of invention.

The first part is happy and youthful, full of exciting contrasts. In the second part, dance rhythms prevail. The trio is a whirling dance, a *springar* from some remote Norwegian valley. Ideas and fancies crowd thick on one another, mood and melody changing like the shifting clouds in a summer sky. The sonata ends in a brilliant *presto,* as wild and unrestrained as the peasants dancing at a wedding or round the bonfires on Midsummer's Eve.

Grieg took his two sonatas to Gade at Klampenborg. He followed Gade up the steep stairs to the Danish musician's studio, and Gade played the compositions. This time Gade, who had expressed moderate praise of the first movement of Grieg's symphony a year before, the same Gade who had found little to his liking in the *Humoresques,* emptied four bottles of water in his enthusiasm over the sonatas. Grieg returned to Rungsted a very happy young man.

Grieg once explained his almost pathetic striving for Gade's approval. "That I was a young beginner and he the famous master must always be remembered in these little stories."

During that happy summer at Rungsted, Grieg composed a song of rich moods and intense feeling for nature. This song was called *Autumn Storm* and was published later as one of the songs of Opus 18.

There is little of the Norwegian coloring in this composition; for Grieg was able to adapt his music to the mood of the Danish poet, Christian Richardt, who wrote the words. With poet and composer we move through the havoc wrought in the Danish landscape by autumn's storms, from the first attack of the winter wind:

"When Storm on his great horn a loud blast blows,
    Through the thickest of leaf-walls a trembling goes."

The storm blows up and changes the "wood's green hat" to yellow and red and brown. Finally the land lies bare and shivering:

"One autumn night is the world laid waste,
    Grim winter's banner is raised in haste
    O'er a desolate land, where his icy breath
    Many a fair tree had doomed to death."

But no matter how bitter the sky or how raw the wind, spring is sure to follow winter. The song ends with the yearning for the first days of spring:

"What has the earth more fair to show
    Than first flower blooming in latest snow!"

The piano introduction of *Autumn Storm* shows with what sure touch Grieg could evoke a mood with his strange harmonies.*

That summer at Rungsted was one of the happiest of Grieg's life. Not only had the longed-for creative mood brought him satisfaction, but also his daily life was enriched by varied experiences and impressions. Friends from Copenhagen came to Rungsted to make trips with Grieg and Feddersen to the parklike groves near the village. Grieg's brother John visited him on his way to Dresden. The great poet of Norway, Björnstjerne Björnson, came out to see the musical genius of whom Nordraak spoke so warmly in every letter. The unhappy matter of parental opposition of his engagement to Nina was also righting itself, and on July 2 of that summer of 1865 the betrothal was publicly announced at an affair nearly as solemn as a marriage ceremony.

When the summer was over it was decided that Grieg should go south for the winter. His father wrote him:

"When you write from Germany, telling me where you propose to spend the winter, I will write further as to how much you will have to manage on; meantime you have something to begin the winter with. You are a costly chap!—in every way—there is no doubt about it."

Before Grieg left Denmark for this winter in the south he wrote several songs to poems of Andreas Munch. One of these was the famous *Cradle Song,* No. 2 of Opus 9. Another was called *Outward Bound,* which might have been intended as a farewell to the pleasant scenes of Den-

* See Appendix, page 245.

mark by one who realized that of perfect things there is always only one, that the perfect summer at Rungsted would never be repeated.

"The morn was dawning in summer skies,
    A ship at anchorage lay,
Where fir trees tall and majestic rise,
    Reflected upon the bay.
The radiant dawnlight was near its birth,
    And into one fragrance blent
Were ocean's breeze and breath of earth
    To make here a stronger scent.

"The somber ship that lay rocking there,
    With tapering masts and high,
Raised the anchor, then laid bare
    Her canvas to the sky.
Oh, see, the golden sun doth rise,
    To gleam on yon mountain peak—
As forth from the harbor the swift bark flies,
    Brighter, sunnier harbors to seek."

The opening soft, slurred chords of the piano and the rocking rhythms* depict a boat at anchor in some northern harbor, waiting to make the journey into the wide, lonely sea.

* See Appendix, page 246.

Chapter Twelve

*I*N SEPTEMBER, following that happy summer of 1865, Grieg set out for Germany. He arrived in Berlin to find his friend Nordraak very ill. Together with Edmund Neupert, the Norwegian concert-pianist, he visited Nordraak every day during the last part of September and the month of October. Nordraak did not rally from his illness, a violent inflammation of the lungs which developed rapidly into tuberculosis. And every day the sad truth was more evident—that the gay, laughing Nordraak had come to grips with something stronger than his eager youth.

November and the cold rains of fall arrived together. The austere buildings and chill squares where the trees stood naked and gray after the frosts, damped Grieg's spirits. He was relieved to have an excuse for getting away from the cold northern city of Germany—even though Leipzig, where his two sonatas were to be performed at a Gewandhaus concert on November 6, was scarcely less cold and forbidding in the fall of the year.

"You will return soon?" begged the sick Nordraak, holding his friend's hand and looking up at him appealingly.

"Of course, of course. And when I come back to Berlin you must be well enough to go to Italy with me." Grieg was all confidence, and Nordraak took heart again.

But Grieg did not return to Nordraak. He wrote instead to his ailing friend of the success of the Gewandhaus concert. Nordraak, sitting propped up with pillows, wrote shakily in his diary:

"Grieg's letter yesterday describes his performance of his piano sonata and his sonata for piano and violin at the evening entertainment in the Gewandhaus in Leipzig. A tremendous success. Encored. How I am looking forward to his coming."

Still Grieg dallied in Leipzig. Nordraak, sick to death in Berlin, rallied his failing strength enough to write an appealing letter, which ended:

"Now you must come, Grieg. Don't delay any longer. I must have you again. Write immediately when you receive these few lines to say that you are coming at once to your devoted

"RIKARD NORDRAAK"

But healthy youth is thoughtless, and young Grieg did

not read the pathos that went into the writing of those lines. On November 30, Nordraak received a letter saying that Grieg had found another companion and was going south to Italy without returning to Berlin at all.

Nordraak was deeply hurt. The letter he wrote in answer to Grieg's announcement of the change of plans was bitter and full of reproaches. It was with perhaps a tiny feeling of guilt that Grieg traveled on to sunny Italy, leaving his dearest friend to fight a lonely battle with illness and despair.

In Italy all was sunshine and gaiety. All the great northern artists spent their winters in Rome if they could. Indeed, Rome was the winter capital of art for the whole world; great and famous men met in clubs to discuss their plans and their philosophies, and distinguished artists appeared every evening in the operas and orchestral concerts.

In Rome Grieg went often to the Scandinavian Club. There he met Henrik Ibsen. At this time the celebrated poet of Norway had turned his back on his native land, which would not grant him the recognition he felt he deserved. He was bitter, and talked often to Grieg of the low standards of culture in their country.

"But what can you expect?" Grieg would argue. "For more than four hundred years Norway was a subject nation to Denmark. And now the Swedes have us under their thumb. How could Norwegians be themselves, with the Danish tongue thrust upon them, and their music and folk tales laughed to scorn by the 'superior' Danish and Swedish aristocracy?"

"There is truth in what you say," Ibsen would growl and look sour.

"Do you know," Grieg would go on, "Norse music was never heard in my mother's drawing-room. Like all other Norwegians, our family believed that only the music imported from other countries had any merit. What had we poor Norwegians done for art? Our attempts excited only pity or caused embarrassment in the fashionable drawing-room."

"Yet," pointed out Ibsen, "Ole Bull showed them what our native fiddlers could do. Even the wealthy and middle-class Norwegians admitted for a short time that the peasant *hallings* and *gangars* and *springars* were dances worth listening to. Ah, they are blind! And deaf! We threw our truth to them, and they turned away like swine before pearls, after a brief look out of curiosity."

"Some day," declared Grieg, "I shall prove to you that the Norwegians have not forgotten their old culture. It is merely dormant. We must turn to the isolated farms and villages where in a land of snow and rain and ice and long winter twilights our people have entertained themselves for centuries with the old stories and the old songs. Nurses and grandmothers keep on telling the little ones about the magic land 'East o' the Sun and West o' the Moon,' and the hardingfeles still play the old songs at weddings and feast days and wakes. You'll see—we'll make the public understand what treasures lie in our own Norwegian mountains and valleys yet."

"The optimism of youth!" laughed Ibsen. "You may be sure I shall be glad if this miracle is accomplished, but

—here, I'll write my ideas in your autograph book."
Smiling his cynical smile, he wrote:

> "Orpheus woke with crystal tones
>   Souls in brutes; struck fire from stones.
>   Stones there are in Norway plenty;
>   Brutes far more than ten or twenty.
>   Play, so stones spark far and wide!
>   Play, to pierce the brute's thick hide!"

"You are much too hard on us, my dear Herr Ibsen,"
laughed Grieg, taking his book again. "I think I shall take
your dare. Energy is the main thing, and I shall work to
make Norway and the world conscious of the rich treas-
ure-house of Norse melody, though my back breaks. That
about the back is an expression of my mother's," he added,
seeing Ibsen's quizzical look at the odd expression.

With Ibsen, Grieg took many walks and drives around
the city of Rome, admiring the art treasures and exploring
the historic ruins. He went often to the banks of the Tiber,
river of a thousand dark stories and ugly secrets, and to
the Forum and other monuments to a past grandeur. He
visited St. Peter's and St. John Lateran, and drove past the
gates of the Vatican.

Best of all, he liked to go in the evening to the Pincio,
known in ancient times as the "Hill of the Gardens." At
this fashionable resort, swarming with people and gay
with youthful laughter and light dance music, Grieg sat
sipping good Italian wine, watching the mists from the
Tiber creep up to cover the domes of the city below.
Sights and sounds of the Pincio were to be set down many

years later in a song written to words of the poet Björnson.

During this winter in Rome, Grieg's creative talent asserted itself in very little original work. Perhaps the thought of Nordraak lying neglected and lonely in the North depressed his spirits. He did, however, make his first use of the orchestra as an instrument. He wrote the overture *In Autumn*, from material taken from his song "Autumn Storm."

In Autumn, published as Opus 11, is music unmistakably Norse in tone. There is humor in it, but gaiety is never far removed from melancholy; such is the character of Norway, now feverishly gay, now gloomy and dark with foreboding. The merry parts of the overture were thought by many to represent the coming of spring after the dark winter—a thought suggested by the ending of the song. Grieg corrected this impression in a letter to a Swiss friend:

"In the overture, the contrasts, poetic as well as musical, are formed by the motive from the song which represents the autumn storm and the merry reaping song of the peasants. There is no suggestion of the coming of the spring in the overture; but there is of a union of the serious and merry elements which characterize the autumn."

In the gay melody which forms the *Allegretto marcato* portion of the overture, a folk tone is imparted to the music by the use of the drone bass. A few bars of this part of the overture, arranged for piano, show the strange bagpipe effect produced by having the same notes in the bass sound over and over again.*

* See Appendix, page 246.

On the 26th of March, Nordraak, far from home and family, lost the struggle with illness. He was buried in the Jerusalemer Kirchhof in Berlin. The news came as a terrible shock to Grieg in Rome. Mourning for his friend, his heart made heavier by the thought that he should not have left him alone during the winter, Grieg wrote his *Funeral March for Nordraak.**

In this composition, Grieg gives expression to his grief in chords which are almost unbearable outbursts of pain. The march was always a favorite of Grieg's. Wherever he went in later years, he carried it with him, and morbidly decided that it should be played at his own funeral. Subconsciously, he may have been trying to atone for his unkindness to his sick friend by carrying with him a perpetual reminder of Nordraak's death.

In May, Grieg returned to Berlin. It seemed to him that all the carefree joy of his life was behind him. With the passing of the exuberant Nordraak a leaf in the book of Grieg's life had turned. He feared that the new pages would not have the same gladsome moods of the past.

Grieg visited Nordraak's grave. Writing to his friend's father, he said: "Do not think that what he yearned after shall be forgotten; it is my great task to make known his few works of genius to the people—to the Norwegian people—to fight for their recognition and build upon their strong foundation." And after his signature he wrote: "The enclosed leaf is from Rikard's grave at the Jerusalemer Kirchhof. It lies in an open and beautiful position, looking out to the city."

* See Appendix, page 265.

With sad thoughts for company, he made his way back to Denmark, where his sympathetic friends and Nina awaited his arrival. All summer Grieg roamed the hills and explored the little woods near Copenhagen. In his room he toiled at his music. With Gottfred Matthison-Hansen he studied the organ, working to prepare himself for a hoped-for position in a church in Christiania. His father wrote to say that he should not pin his hopes on getting the position, that the church in question was not yet built. He applied for a position in the National Theater in Christiania and did not get the job. It was in gloomy mood, therefore, that he went out to Klampen-borg to see Gade.

Grieg took his *In Autumn* overture for the master's approval; but Gade only snorted, "This is trash, Grieg; go home and write something better."

Grieg went home and wept. Everything was different, he reflected bitterly. The golden days when he and Nordraak had talked over their high dreams for Norse music, the exciting days when they organized the Euterpe, the genial days at Rungsted, when pent-up genius had gushed forth in works that won the great Gade's favor, seemed at an end.

But this black mood passed. In a chastened spirit, he decided that Gade's judgment was partially right. The overture was poorly orchestrated as it stood. Grieg arranged the overture as a duet, which he played with Nina. Years later he reorchestrated the overture, and in this form it was finally published, in 1887.

The duet arrangement of *In Autumn* he sent to a com-

petition arranged by the Swedish Academy. Gade, who
was one of the judges, must have forgotten all about calling the work "trash"; for he voted with the other judges
to give it first prize. Thus Grieg had his little revenge on
the great master.

With the coming of fall, Grieg bade his winsome Nina
goodbye. The time had come, he decided, when he must
make a start in Christiania. He planned a concert, which
would introduce him to the public, and then he would
earn his living by teaching.

Some weeks later, Nina came to Norway with Madame
Norman-Neruda to take part in this concert on October
15. Grieg played his piano sonata and his *Humoresques,*
and with Fru Norman-Neruda, the eminent violinist, he
presented his violin sonata. Nina sang songs by Kjerulf
and Nordraak, and some of Grieg's own.

The concert was a huge success. Music critics of the
Christiania newspapers were generous with their praise.
It was with a lighter heart that Grieg said a second
goodbye to Nina. There was every prospect that he would
be a success in Christiania. This meant that their marriage
could be arranged before long.

The family in Bergen, waiting anxiously for word from
Edvard, received a telegram telling of his success. His
mother, who seldom took up her pen, wrote him an affec-
tionate note:

"I must send you a few lines to tell you how deeply
happy and thankful I am over your success. A thing like
that is exalting: it puts you into the frame of mind that
is essential if you are to make the most of yourself in

the situation in life you desire to reach." She ended the letter with a jesting reproof: "But Edvard, you wretch, how could you put us off with a telegram? You know so well—all too well—how dear you are to us. Cannot that knowledge wake a kindred feeling, a desire to let us know in some detail as quickly as possible all that concerns you?"

His favorite sister Elisabeth wrote to tell him of the excitement his telegram caused. Father, she said, was nearly out of his head with joy. He ran from room to room to tell the family the good news—into the drawing-room to tell Elisabeth, into the kitchen to find Mother, up to the attic to tell John. "A thousand congratulations, dear Edvard," she closed. "I cannot tell you how absolutely delighted I am."

Thus encouraged by praise from the critics of Christiania, warm congratulations from his family, and the approval of lovely Nina, Grieg opened his studio and hung out his sign to say that he would teach students of the piano. He adjusted himself hopefully to a new life of hard work and exacting routine in the cold eastern city of Norway.

Chapter Thirteen

Jack shall have Jill;
Nought shall go ill . . ."
A MIDSUMMER NIGHT'S DREAM

THE doubts and discouragements of the summer were
put aside as Grieg seriously took up his duties in November. The musical public of Christiania accepted him
hospitably, and he soon had more pupils than he could
teach. The Harmonic Society appointed him conductor.
Winter-Hjelm sought his help in founding a Norwegian
Academy of Music.

Grieg often had occasion to remember Ibsen's words
about the low cultural standard of the Norwegian public.
At concerts many in the audience would rudely rise before the last composition was played to its close, spoiling

the enjoyment of the others by scraping their chairs, rustling their programs, and whispering "Excuse me" and "If you please" as they passed into the aisles. Grieg's indignation led him to insert in the newspaper, on behalf of the Philharmonic concerts, a notice requesting the prospective audience "to put their cloaks, coats, and other encumbrances out of their minds during the finale of the symphony [Beethoven's Fifth] and to remain in their seats till the last bar, so that everybody may have the pleasure of hearing this brilliant piece of music to the end."

True to his promise to Nordraak's father and to himself, Grieg produced several of his dead friend's works in Christiania that winter. In a letter to Emil Hornemann in Denmark he wrote: *"Sigurd Slembe* created a tremendous furore . . . You should have heard our students' choir. This was something altogether different from the performance in Denmark. It gripped me so strongly as I conducted that a kind of shudder went through me."

In May, with a successful musical season behind him, Grieg was already worrying about his composing. Again he wrote his friend Hornemann: "You have worked like a horse at Euterpe this winter—though not harder than I at the Philharmonic here. And I have besides the Academy and private teaching. It is not difficult to see what is to become of the composer. But wait—that will come all right."

Thrusting aside these vague fears that he was sacrificing his talent as a composer to the grim business of making a living, Grieg took stock of his prospects and found them good. He felt at last that he could marry Nina. He wrote their friend Gottfred Matthison-Hansen:

"After a winter brought to a successful conclusion, I am coming back to the green woods happier than I have ever been before. Down there, under the bright arches, I shall meet my little maid, and go with her to church, and from there our course will be laid homeward towards the coast of Norway, where I shall live and work. . . ."

The wedding took place on June 11, 1867, with the parents-in-law in anything but a forgiving mood. Grudgingly they attended the quiet, almost subdued ceremony. Grieg's friend Stenberg, the singer, repeated his old words of encouragement to Fru Hagerup: "Only be patient. One day he will be world-famous!" But Nina's mother did not look convinced.

Nina may have been hurt by her parents' ill will, but Grieg himself had no intention of allowing them to make him angry or depressed. In the gayest spirits in the world he took his young bride off with him to Christiania, where he had already prepared a home at Övre Voldgate 2 IV.

Nina settled contentedly into the plain, modest, comfortable little home, and Grieg in his attic room set himself joyously to composing. In three weeks' time he wrote his second violin sonata, in G major, Opus 13. In spite of the melancholy opening chords, the sonata is in the main buoyant and light-hearted, reflecting Grieg's happiness and delight in life.

In the introductory bars on the piano, there is a typical Grieg combination of chords—octave, seventh, and fifth. Again and again this combination appeared in later compositions, like a signature to identify Grieg's music.

A Norwegian *springdans* forms the theme of the first movement. In the second movement, another folk-dance breaks through the elegiac character of the theme. In this composition it is apparent that Grieg is remembering the lively Bergen folk, the dances around the St. John's bonfires, the weddings and the fairs, the peasants singing for Ole Bull at Osteröen.

At Christmas time the young couple spent the holiday with Björnson and his family, who lived on Rosenkranz Street in Christiania. On Christmas Eve, Nina stowed bundles into the sleigh which Edvard had hired to take them to Björnson's. Edvard tucked Nina under a fur robe as if she had been a package herself, shook the reins, and off they flew through the winter twilight. Lights winked at them from every window, and sleigh-bells made jolly music in the cold air. As the horse trotted briskly through the streets packed with snow Edvard remarked, "This is a regular Dickens Christmas. Father used to read his books to us by the hour. I always liked best the parts about the Christmas parties."

Before they arrived at Rosenkranz, Nina's hair and muff and Edvard's fur cap were dusted over with the powdery flakes sifting from the gray sky. Jolly "Björn," as the poet was called by his friends, met them at the door hung with a *Jul* wreath of holly and evergreen.

"Merry Christmas, merry Christmas, you two young *Jul* brownies," he shouted gaily. "Children," he called over his shoulder, "our guests have arrived. Mother, take Nina under your wing, will you? She looks half frozen."

The Björnsons were large, hearty people. It looked quite funny to see them pulling their little friends the Griegs into the hallway—like two bears welcoming a couple of snowbirds that had come hopping by.

Björnson and his wife and their children celebrated Christmas in the old-fashioned way. In the drawing-room was a huge glittering tree, where the gifts were already piled high. From the kitchen came the most delightful smells to mingle with the forest scent of pine and fir and cedar. Grieg was reminded of those past Christmases in Bergen—at the home in Strandgaten and out at beautiful Landås.

Grieg sniffed the air. *"Mölje!"* he declared wrinkling his short nose in a pleased way.

"Mölje," agreed Björnson. "What would Christmas Eve be without mölje?"

"And gingerbread, I think?" said Nina, taking off her wool mittens to warm her fingers at the huge stove in the corner.

"Gingerbread animals with currant eyes," chorused the children. "We peeked when cook wasn't looking."

"For shame!" said their mother, but her eyes smiled.

Before they were allowed to sit down to the wholesome broth called mölje, Björnson insisted that Grieg play the organ for the Christmas hymn. Björnson placed before him a composition of Grundvig. Grieg sighed when he saw that there were thirty-two verses and that Björnson intended to have the assembled family, servants, and Nina sing them all. Half asleep at the end of verse thirty-two, Grieg was amazed to hear Björnson's booming voice exhorting the singers to "start from the beginning, please"—and the whole thing had to be done again.

After the dinner, the Griegs and the entire Björnson household gathered around the tree. They sang carols, and Björnson handed out the presents. Grieg's present from Björnson was the poet's *Short Pieces.* Björnson's gift from Grieg was a book of *Lyrical Short Pieces,* for piano, Opus 12.

Grieg's book was seized upon by eager hands. As the Björnson household set up a clamor for Grieg to play some of the pieces for them, he sat down at the grand piano.

"This composition," he explained before playing *The Watchman's Song,* "was composed after I had seen a performance of Shakespeare's *Macbeth.*" His sensitive fingers found the notes of the somber little piece, and his hearers imagined they heard the voices of the ghosts in the night and the watchman's shout.*

Next he turned to a dainty work called *Dance of the Elves.* Then in rollicking holiday mood he swung into *Folk-Song* and *Norwegian.*

"Those last two," bellowed the delighted Björnson, "*those* show that you know our peasant life, inside and out."

The last composition of the collection was *Song of the Fatherland.*† The power and sincerity of the emotion expressed in this composition so roused Björnson's enthusiasm that he was on his feet at the close shouting "Bravo!" as if he had been in a theater.

* See Appendix, page 247.
† See Appendix, page 247.

"That is music fit for a Viking," he roared, looking like a Viking himself as he said it. "I shall write words for that music."

Grieg, knowing how busy the poet was, and how in his enthusiasm he was given to blowing hot and cold, did not expect the promised words to be written. However, Björnson was busy with them the very next day, and on the third day he came rushing to Grieg's studio to show him the poem—a "song for the youth of Norway," he called it.

Grieg himself related the amusing story of Björnson's arrival with his song:

"As I sat up in my attic at Övre Voldgate, giving a piano lesson to a young lady, I heard a ring at the door that threatened to bring down the bell, wires and all. Then a rumbling as of wild hordes invading and a bellow: 'Forward! Forward! Hurrah! Now I have it! Forward!' My pupil shook like an aspen leaf. My wife in the next room was frightened out of her wits. But when the door flew open and Björnson stood there beaming like the sun with delight, then there was jubilation. And then we heard that beautiful, just completed poem:

"'Forward! was our fathers' battle cry.
Forward! we, their sons, too shout on high!'"

This song was first sung by the students of Christiania, the following year, in their procession honoring Johann Welhaven, Bergen poet, who wrote of the old Norse subjects.

In the years to come, Grieg and Björnson were to collaborate on many works. Healthy, enthusiastic Björnson was a valued friend in the years spent by Grieg in Christiania. It was Björnson who stood by the young composer through all the storms that broke in the Academy and in the Philharmonic, where the growing envy and malice of musicians and critics who feared Grieg's genius made life more and more difficult for the composer.

In April 1868 a daughter was born to the Griegs. They called her Alexandra, after Grieg's grandfather. The arrival of the baby was greeted by warm congratulations from Edvard's family, who sent much advice for the little one's welfare. Even Nina's mother unbent enough to ask the young parents to leave the baby with her when they came to Denmark in the summer.

In honor of the baby's birth, Grieg wrote his appealing *Margaret's Cradle Song.** The music was set to words of a poem from Ibsen's play *The Pretenders*.

Summer's bright days brought Nina and Edvard to Denmark. When Alexandra had been left with the grandparents, the composer and his wife rented a small house in Sölleröd, a village about an hour's trip from Copenhagen. There, in a gardener's hut, Grieg set up his music workshop.

It was a summer very nearly as satisfying as that earlier summer at Rungsted. Grieg made the most of his vacation from the worries of teaching and conducting in Christiania. He slept late, breakfasted without hurrying, smoked

* See Appendix, page 247.

a cigarette—and then he was off to his piano in the gardener's house.

Sometimes friends would come out and carry Nina away with them for a day of picnicking in the woods. It was strictly understood that Edvard was not to be disturbed at his work. When evening came, however, Edvard closed his piano and joined Nina and their friends at jolly supper parties and gatherings at the local inn.

The chief work of that summer was the *Piano Concerto,* in A minor, Opus 16.* This composition of the twenty-five-year-old composer is thought by many to be his best work. It has been ranked with the great concertos of pianist-composers such as Chopin, Schumann, Rubinstein, and Saint-Saëns.

In this concerto, fresh, virile, sad, and gay by turns, Grieg realized his ambition to write a great piece of music with the Norse coloring. The Concerto in A minor is as Norwegian as the famous Bergen rain, as Ole Bull, as Olaf the Sailor, as the Fishmarket of the Triangle. Norway's deep melancholy, born of long winter twilights and cold and too much work in barren, scanty fields, is in the sad orchestral introduction to the slow movement with its haunting melody. The fall from the seventh of the scale to the fifth, and from the third to the tonic, are progressions encountered often in Northern folk tunes; Grieg knew what he was doing when he opened his concerto with such a phrase. The phrase is carried from A minor into C major—a device which Grieg often used and which gives the music that strange, unearthly

* See Appendix, page 248.

quality peculiar to the folk music of Norway. In one measure there is a "cross-rhythm" of three-notes-to-the-beat against two-notes-to-the-beat—a rhythm characteristic of the peasants' *springdans.*

There is a veritable fireworks display in this composition of Grieg's radically new ideas of harmony. His manner of harmonizing with chromatic sixths or thirds, his love of bare fifths—both find expression in this exotic concerto.

In September Nina and Edvard and Alexandra were back in Christiania. Grieg's work was becoming more and more distasteful to him. His superior talents had roused the envy of almost every musician in town. The Philharmonic seethed with malicious whisperings and silly little plots. The Academy showed signs of being a failure. The Town Council plunged into the mêlée in a stupid and petty way by refusing to allow Grieg a reduction of rent for the use of the Lodge Hall. This hall was required for the four subscription concerts which Grieg gave every year.

There was a general conspiracy against him, it seemed. Just before the concerts were scheduled to take place, the first violins demanded an unheard-of amount of money for their services. Grieg, furious and deeply hurt, showed the stubbornness which was a decided part of his make-up. He gave the concerts without orchestra.

"I was determined now to push my concerts through in some form or other, no matter what—and they went," he wrote to his friend Matthison-Hansen.

One of Björnson's sons, who attended the first of these concerts, whispered to his father: "Grieg looks like a Viking, doesn't he? A little Viking."

A Viking Grieg continued to be, with an indomitable fighting spirit and a belief in himself and the Norse music he was attempting to make known. Nevertheless, he was growing weary of a life of continuous bickering and nasty exchanges with fellow musicians and the critics who were against him.

Writing to a friend in Rome, Grieg spoke of his profound discouragement. His friend turned the letter over to Franz Liszt, who was living in retirement in a monastery near Rome. Liszt, who knew very well what the struggles of a young composer entailed, and whose great delight was to help struggling young artists, sat down immediately and wrote a letter. It was a personal letter to Grieg, praising his sonata for violin, Opus 8.

Liszt, the old fox, knew what he was about. The warm praise in that letter was just the miracle that was needed. Grieg sent it with an application to the Norwegian government for a traveling stipend, and the authorities, properly impressed by the opinions of the man considered to be the world's greatest pianist, granted the honorarium.

Grieg's spirits shot upward like a gas-filled balloon. He was free! Free at least for a year, to travel and compose. No more lessons for a while. No more struggling to keep the Academy going in the face of public indifference. No more ugly quarrels with the Philharmonic musicians, the rabid critics, and the well-fed, musically-ignorant Town Council!

Grieg and Nina smiled to themselves at the change in all these people when it was known that the government had granted a stipend. Turning from coldness and actual malice, the musicians of Christiania began to fawn. Writing to his friend Grönvold, Grieg remarked contemptuously:

"I was the recipient of a rain of undeserved compliments from all sides, utterly mal à propos—in other words, only a result of the compliments imported from Rome."

So it was in festive mood that in April Grieg celebrated his little daughter's first birthday, gave a last concert for the benefit of a memorial to Halfdan Kjerulf, and set out with his family to spend the summer at Landås. Then the plan was to direct their footsteps toward the sunny south, to Rome.

Chapter Fourteen

It was the friar of orders grey . . .
THE TAMING OF THE SHREW

*W*ITH high hopes and jubilant spirits the young Griegs
set out for Landås. After the struggle to earn a living
for his family by teaching, the temporary security of the
traveling stipend was good medicine for Grieg's nervous
system. On the little steamer which took them by the sea
route to Bergen, he laughed and joked and played merrily
with baby Alexandra. Nina, watching the two of them,
smiled her mysterious smile. Quiet, shy Nina had many
a private joke; perhaps that is why the laugh wrinkles
showed at the corner of her eyes though she seldom
laughed outright.

Their happiness was to receive a rude jolt, however.
They had scarcely settled themselves in their comfortable

rooms at Landås when little Alexandra took sick. The baby responded to no medical treatment, and quite suddenly died in her thirteenth month. Nina was stunned by the cruel blow. Like Gudrun of old, she sat dry-eyed, bottling up her sorrow within her.

"A terrible thing," fumed Father Grieg. "What a terrible thing for a young couple to bear!"

Mother Grieg nodded silently, following Nina's pathetic movements about the house with pitying eyes.

As for Edvard, he locked himself in his workroom with his grief. He would not accept sympathy. Savagely he played, raging at life which at one moment lifted him up only to plunge him down again into despair. He thought of that time at school when he had brought his little attempt at composition, and the teacher, first pretending to praise him, had then humiliated him before his classmates. "So near the peak of happiness and then in a moment down in the depths! How often has it been like that for me in life. And every time my thoughts have gone back involuntarily to this first time."

Music, which had comforted Edvard after Nordraak's death, brought solace again. In *Among Roses,* a song to Kristofer Janson's poem, he poured out his sorrow. It was like sharing a burden of grief by speaking of it to an understanding friend, this putting of his emotion into song. When the composition was written down at last, the keen edge of the composer's sorrow had been dulled, and he could take up his life and his work with confidence again.

Roaming over the heather-and-birch-covered hills and

walking along the old waterfront of the Tyskebrygge, Grieg began to feel the urge to create. Some poems of Hans Christian Andersen came to mind, and these he set to music, in the evenings and early mornings, locked in his workroom. These eight songs were published as Opus 18. *Woodland Wandering* was the first of the *Eight Songs*—a gay and charming piece in which Grieg for a moment recaptured the zest of the youthful days in Denmark. *Autumn Storm,* the song written during the happy period of inspiration following the meeting with Nordraak, was included in this opus.

Before he left Landås, Grieg came into contact with a collection of folk music which opened the doors at last to the authentic treasures of Norse melody. This was the Lindeman collection of *Old and New Mountain Melodies.* Using some of the tunes of this collection, Grieg wrote the twenty-five dances and songs of his Opus 17, dedicated to Ole Bull. This was the first time that Grieg used folk material not merely as an inspiration for his art but also as a foundation for his composition. In the process of converting the old tunes into songs, dances, and tone poems of more conventional form, Grieg showed his genius for taking the raw material of the folk music, moulding it and smoothing it as a potter would the clay of his native hillsides, and presenting to the world a finished art product infused with his own personality.

In the autumn of 1869, Grieg and his wife set out for Copenhagen on their way to Italy.

"It seems as if with the falling of the leaves and the

restless moving of the servant girls on *flyttledag* our own nestlings always fly away. You are regular birds of passage," sighed Mother Grieg.

Edvard, noticing with dismay his mother's graying hair and her tired eyes, whispered, "You must not work so hard. You must rest more."

"My dear boy, you might as well ask your mother to take to an invalid's chair," declared his father, who had overheard. "She *will* work—cooking and baking, knitting, housecleaning, gracious knows what! None of these things can be done properly by the servants, it seems."

Mother Grieg smiled, but her eyes had the far-away dreamy look which Edvard had grown to recognize as a part of her. He suspected that his mother was not always so happy as she pretended, and that work and duty filled an empty place in her life.

"She lives a life of her own, within herself, and no one is allowed to share it," commented Nina to Edvard as the carriage whisked them away from the waving family.

"She has courage. It is not her way to whimper or complain," declared Edvard thoughtfully.

In Copenhagen, the Griegs gave two concerts. Nina sang her husband's songs in her charming, simple way, with feeling but without affectation. She appeared as she always had, without makeup, without flowers and jewelry, in a simple frock. Her hair, short and curly like a child's, gave her a piquant look, and her wide eyes held a look of combined sauciness and gentle sympathy which won her public immediately.

All her life Nina sang her husband's songs; yet the

thought that her sweet, clear voice should earn her a
place as an independent artist seems never to have entered
her head. Grieg's attitude toward his wife was the typical
protective, possessive, and slightly patronizing one of
the nineteenth-century husband, but Nina seems not to
have minded. Her days were spent making Edvard's life
comfortable, in saving him from the petty annoyances of
everyday living, in being a charming hostess to his friends
and a tactful mediator in cases where Grieg's sudden
temper and stubborn opinions were likely to bring him
into conflict with other artists and with the critics.
Charming, sincere, talented, Nina Grieg was the true
artist, as skilled in the art of living as in the art of music.

The concerts in the hall of the Casino in Copenhagen
were a success. After visiting the good friends of Copenhagen and Rungsted and Klampenborg, the Griegs made
the journey to Rome.

It was Grieg's intention to call on Franz Liszt at the
monastery where the great Hungarian was an abbé; but
he had no notion how soon this opportunity was to come
to him. In his letters to his parents, Grieg gave a vivid
description of his meeting with the most famous pianist
of the day:

"Rome, Feb. 17, 1870.

"Dear Parents!

"This morning we were to have gone out with several
Scandinavians to Tivoli for a few days, but what do you
think happened? Yesterday afternoon, as I was sitting in
the Scandinavian Club playing Whist, in came Sgambati
—a very fine pianist, I think I have spoken of him—

bringing a message from Liszt that he would like to see
me at his house the next morning at 11 o'clock. Though
I had been looking forward very much to the Tivoli
tour, this came first naturally, and the plan was changed.
This wasn't, however, my first meeting with Liszt—as
you shall now hear. He has, since the beginning of the
Council (he can't bear either it or its principles), gone
back to Tivoli, where he resides in the Villa d'Este. Very
rarely he comes to town, and on one such occasion I got
to know that he was here, went right away to see him,
did not meet him, and left my card. A couple of days
later he went away, but just then I met Ravnkilde, the
Danish musician, who lives here; he told me that he had
just had a note from a German painter whom Liszt had
asked to find me out through Ravnkilde. He was to tell
me that Liszt was extremely sorry that he had not had
time to look me up and to ask if I would come to see
him the next morning at 10. He was in town and expect-
ing me. I rushed out to him. He lives close to the Titus
Triumphal Arch and the old Roman Forum, in a monastery. But Ravnkilde had told me that Liszt likes people
to bring something with them and, alas! my best compositions have been either at home or in Germany for some
time now. I had to rush up to Winding, to whom I had
presented earlier a copy of my last violin sonata, and
play 'Giver-giver—taker back.' Winding kept the en-
velope, I took the contents, wrote on the outside 'To Dr.
F. Liszt with admiration'—took besides under my arm
my funeral march for Nordraak and a booklet of songs
(the one with 'Outward Bound' in it) and hurried down

the street, with a little qualm at my stomach I won't deny, but that I could have spared myself; for a more lovable man than Liszt it would hardly be possible to find.

"He came smilingly towards me and said in the most genial way, 'We have corresponded a little, have we not?' I told him that I had his letter to thank for being where I was, which drew from him a roar of laughter like that of Ole Bull. All the while his eyes, with a certain ravenous expression in them, were fixed on the packet I had under my arm. Ha, ha, I thought, Ravnkilde was right. And his long, spider-like fingers approached to such an alarming degree that I thought it wisest to set about opening the packet at once. He began to turn over the leaves, that is to say, he read the first part of the sonata through cursorily, and that there was no humbug about the reading was shown by the significant nod, 'Bravo' or 'Very beautiful!' with which he marked the best bits. My spirits began to soar; but when he now asked me to play the sonata my courage altogether failed me. I had never before tried to put the whole thing together for the piano and I would gladly have escaped having to sit and make a mess of it before him. But there was no help for it.

"So I began on his beautiful grand piano (Chickering). Right at the beginning, where the violin breaks in with a little baroque but national passage, he broke out, 'Ah, how full of life! Now, let me tell you, that pleases me! Once again, please!' And when the violin the second time slips into the adagio, he played the violin part higher up on the piano in octaves with such beautiful expression, so remarkably true and singing that I smiled inwardly. These were the first notes I heard from Liszt. And now we went dashing into the allegro, he the violin, I the piano. I got more and more into form, I was so happy over his applause, which in truth flowed so copiously that I felt the most singular thankfulness streaming through me. When the first part was over, I asked him if I might play something for the piano alone and chose the Minuet from the Humoresques, which you no doubt remember.

"When I had played the first eight bars and repeated them he sang the melody with me and did it with an air of heroic power in his bearing that I entirely understood. I saw very well that it was its national character that appealed to him. I had guessed it would be so and had therefore taken things with me in which I had attempted to pluck the national string. When the Minuet was over I felt that, if there was to be any question of getting Liszt to play, it must be now when he was obviously in great spirits. I asked him and he shrugged his shoulders slightly; but when I said that he couldn't let me leave the South without having heard a note from him, he mumbled, with a little flourish, 'Well, I'll play what you wish—I am not like that!' and in a second he had out a score which he had just completed, a kind of ecclesiastical processional march to Tasso's grave, a supplement to his famous symphonic poem for orchestra—*Tasso, Lamento e Trionfo*. Then down he sat and set the keys in motion. I assure you that he belched out, if I may use so unbeautiful an expression, one mass of fire and fervor, one vivid thought after another. It sounded as if he were invoking Tasso's spirit. He paints in garish colors, but a subject like this is just for him; to portray tragic greatness is his strength. I did not know which to admire more, the composer or the pianist; for his playing was magnificent. He doesn't exactly play—one forgets that he is a musician; he becomes a prophet who announces the Day of Judgment so that all the spirits of the universe quiver under his fingers. He invades the most secret places of the soul and delves one's innermost being with demoniac power.

"When that was over, Liszt said quite casually, 'Now, we shall go further into the sonata!' and I, naturally, 'No, thanks very much. After that I shouldn't like to.' But now comes the best. Says Liszt, 'But why not? Give it here. I will do it.' Now remember, first he didn't know the sonata, had never heard or seen it before, and second, it was a violin sonata with a violin part that develops independently of the piano, now above, now below. And what did Liszt do? He played the whole affair, lock, stock, and barrel, violin, piano, nay more, for he played with more fullness and breadth. The violin was given its due right in the middle of the piano part, he was literally all over the whole piano at the same time, without a note being missed. And how, then, did he play? With majesty, beauty, genius beyond compare in interpretation. I believe I laughed, laughed like an idiot. And when I stammered some words of admiration he mumbled, 'Well, you could expect that of me, to read something at sight. I'm an old hand at the game.'—Wasn't it all gra-

cious and kind from first to last? No other big man I
have met has been like him. Then finally I played the
funeral march, which also was to his taste, then I talked
a little with him about all sorts of things—told him
among other things that my father had heard him in
London in 1824, which pleased him. 'Yes, yes, I have
concertized much in the world, too much,' he said. Then
I took my leave and made my way home, wonderfully
hot in the head but conscious that I had spent two of the
most interesting hours of my life. And now I am asked
to go to him again tomorrow and naturally I am delighted.

"The day after the visit I have just described for you,
the Italians Sgambati and Pinelli (pupils of Joachim)
played my first violin sonata at a matinée where the
whole fashionable world was present. Liszt came in the
middle of the concert, just before my sonata, and that
was well. For I do not put down the applause the sonata
received to my own account. The thing is that when Liszt
claps they all clap—each louder than the other."

In a second letter Grieg described another visit with
Liszt:

"Rome, April 9, 1870.

"Dear Parents,

"This time I can say in earnest: where shall I begin
or end! All my impressions and experiences swarm together in my brain in one stupendous chaos. The best
thing will be to give a biographical sketch of the weeks
just passed. First I must give you an account of my
second visit to Liszt, which took place soon after I had

sent my previous letter and was in no way behind the first in interest. Fortunately I had just received from Leipzig the manuscript of my piano concerto and this I took with me. Besides me there were present Winding, Sgambati, and a German Lisztian, unknown to me, who carried plagiarism so far as to wear the dress of an abbé; then there was a Chevalier de Concilium, and a few young ladies of the kind that would like to eat Liszt up, with hair and hide. Their admiration is simply comic. . . .

"Winding and I were very anxious to see if he would really play my concerto at sight. For my part I thought it an impossibility. Liszt, however, thought otherwise. He said, 'Will you play?' I excused myself with a 'No—I cannot' (I have never so far practised it). So Liszt took the manuscript, went to the piano, and said with his own particular smile addressed to all present, 'Now I will show you that I too cannot.' Then he began. I admit that he took the first part of the concerto rather too quickly and the beginning lost a little by it, but later, when I made an opportunity to indicate the time myself, he played as only he and none other can play. It is characteristic that the cadenza, which is technically extremely difficult, he played perfectly. His dramatic gestures are beyond words. He does not rest content with playing only—no, he talks and criticises at the same time. He flings brilliant remarks now to one, now to another in the company, deals out significant nods to right and left, most when something pleases him especially. In the adagio and even more in the finale he reached his culminating point in regard both to execution and to the praise he gave.

"I must not forget a really divine episode. Towards the end of the finale the second theme is repeated, as you will remember, in a grand fortissimo. In the preceding bars, where the first note of the theme's first triplets, G sharp, changes to G in the orchestra, while the piano in a tremendous scale figure traverses all its range of keys, he stopped suddenly, rose to his full height, left the piano and paced with stalwart, theatrical step and arm uplifted through the great hall of the monastery while he fairly bellowed the theme. At the G I have spoken of, he stretched out his arm commandingly like an emperor and shouted, 'G, G, not G sharp! Wonderful! That is just like Swedish Bank!' and then, as if in parenthesis, almost pianissimo, 'Smetana has lately sent me something of that sort.' Then he went back to the piano, repeated the whole strophe, and finished off. At the end he said with a singularly cordial accent as he handed me the book: 'Go ahead. I tell you, you have the talent for it, and—don't let them intimidate you!' This last has infinite importance for me. There is something I will call consecrated in it. Often, when disappointment and bitterness come, I will think of his words, and that the remembrance of this moment will have a wonderful power to sustain me in days of adversity, I firmly believe."

Before leaving Rome, Grieg made hasty outlines of three significant compositions: *Mountain Dance, The Bridal Procession Passes,* and *From the Carnival,* published later as *Sketches of Norwegian Life,* for piano, Opus 19.

The last piece, *From the Carnival,* was inspired by the gay mood of an Italian street celebration, but the first two are purely Norwegian.

The Bridal Procession Passes is Grieg at his best, in his most "Norwegian mood." The subtle impressionism of this piece guides us into a wonderland of harmony, melody, and rhythm, where rapidly shifting scenes appear before us: The faraway music of fiddlers, the bridal party in boats on the fjord gaily making for shore, the forming of the procession to the church—bride and groom in costume at the head and all the villagers following with music and singing and laughter—the distant peal of bells, the passing of the bridal party into the distance, the fading into silence of their music and laughter. In this composition, Grieg is pointing the way to the impressionists, who twenty years later were to use just these same devices of color, movement, rhythm, and contrast in their music. Both Ravel and Debussy studied Grieg's harmony with profit. And the American Mac-Dowell admired Grieg's work so much that he dedicated two of his own works to the eminent Norwegian; these were MacDowell's sonatas, the *Keltic* (Opus 59) and the *Norse* (Opus 57).

The first eight bars and the last sixteen bars* of *The Bridal Procession Passes* show Grieg's genius in creating moods and painting pictures through music.

After a spring in Naples, Grieg and his wife turned

* See Appendix, page 248.

toward the North again. A brief stay in Denmark, and they were on their way to spend the summer in Landås. Their spirits were cheerful once again. Music and time had softened the blow of Alexandra's death. There were no very unhappy memories waiting for them on the doorstep, where Mother Grieg and Father Grieg stood waving a welcome.

Chapter Fifteen

He that is thy friend indeed,
He will help thee in thy need:
THE PASSIONATE PILGRIM

THE summer at Landås was the last of the vacation from the duties in Christiania. In the little workroom Grieg completed the *Sketches of Norwegian Life* begun in Rome. He tried to solve the problem of finding a publisher who would take all his future works, but had slight success. It was not until he made an agreement years later with the famous Peters firm of Leipzig that Grieg's publishing difficulties were ended. When Dr. Max Abraham leased the firm in the late '80s, Grieg, along with many another composer, came to rest in "Father Abraham's bosom," as one artist put it, and was able to work under secure financial conditions.

With serious misgivings, Grieg returned to Christiania.

In September 1870 he began work by giving a concert of his own and Nordraak's works. Stubbornly refusing to be intimidated by the petty backbiting that started as soon as he was back in harness, he proposed the founding of a Musical Society. Grimly he sank his teeth in the project, like a terrier in some coveted piece of cloth, and hung on until he accomplished his purpose by October of the following year. With the organization of the Musical Society, orchestral music in Christiania was placed on a firmer and more permanent basis.

Teaching, giving concerts, Grieg pursued his lonely way. Sometimes the discouragement of working for an unappreciated idea was almost too great. His fighting spirit could not be downed, however. To the music-dealer Hagen, he wrote:

"Send me a breath of fresh air . . . and if you see any criticisms of my things be sure to send them too. I want folks here to know that intellect is appreciated amongst you people. . . . The thing is, the philistines who control the artistic press here have unanimously made up their minds to do me down by silence. But they won't manage it. So certainly as I write from the bottom of my heart, so certainly my work will struggle through."

Among all these enemies of his music, Grieg did not find one who was willing to be in the least fair to his work. There was one true friend in Christiania, however, who helped the composer in many ways during the eight years spent in the eastern city. This friend was Björnson. "He was a true friend to me in those years," Grieg once

wrote to his friend Holter. "Although he did not understand music, he believed in me."

Björnson offered encouragement not merely in the form
of words but also in more practical ways. Whenever there
was a festival or regatta or memorial service in honor of
some great man, it was the custom for those in charge
to order a suitable piece of music for the occasion. Much
of this music was designed for choral singing, requiring
a poem as well as music. Björnson was invariably com-
missioned to write the poem, and he saw to it that his
struggling young friend Grieg received the commission
to set his words to music. Thus many a sorely needed
sum of money came to the composer. This association
with Björnson accounts for the fact that most of Grieg's
music during the Christiania years was a series of settings
for Björnson's poetry.

"How about some music for Independence Day?"
Björnson came shouting up the stairway one evening.
"My play *Sigurd Jorsalfar* [*Sigurd the Crusader*] will be
presented. Your job will be to set it to music—parts of
it, anyway. Now here is what I suggest—" and hearty
Björnson, whose enormous vitality enabled him to stick
to a task for endless hours, laid out enough work for ten
composers.

Grieg set to work to make a deadline an incredibly
few days away. As usual, when he had made up his mind,
he stuck stubbornly to the task, and on the appointed
May 17, 1872, the music was ready. He had had but
eight days to compose and orchestrate the score.

The play was produced at the Christiania Theater.

With Grieg's musical setting it was a huge success. It was a colorful, stirring folk-drama, a play with the very moods and scenes best calculated to rouse Grieg's finest creative mood.

The music for the play consisted of a quiet introduction, two marches, and two songs for baritone solo, male choir, and orchestra. The songs were later published as Opus 22, and the marches and introduction arranged as a suite for orchestra and published as Opus 56.

Björnson did not hear the work until its second performance, the next year. Grieg persuaded him to go to the theater, where composer and poet sat together, close to the stage. All the Björnson children sat high in the balcony to hear the work, too.

Grieg, knowing that many of the performers were poor singers, whispered to Björnson, "Some of this may be rather painful, Björn."

They watched with interest the scene on the stage depicting Borghild's uneasy sleep. Her restless dreams were suggested by Grieg's agitated music, which grew more and more sinister to indicate dread and fear.

The introduction to the second act, wherein the two kings, Sigurd and Öistjen, display their swordsmanship in a trial of strength, was virile music, colorful and barbaric, in harmony with the subject. A proud, strong theme portrayed King Sigurd; the dignified but milder and weaker theme of the middle movement portrayed King Öistjen.

"Something approaching the Wagnerian *leitmotif* is

made use of here, isn't it, Grieg?" Björnson whispered.

The triumphal March, an inspired tone poem, had Björnson and the rest of the audience sitting straight in their seats. As the two kings walked on the stage, hand in hand, the principal theme was played softly by a quartet of 'cellos. The theme was taken up by the violins and carried on by the horns and woodwinds. At the point where the halberdiers entered in pairs and placed themselves on both sides of the steps, the tuba and the bassoon took the lead. Little by little, the whole orchestra joined in as the hordes of Normans welcomed the kings with crashing shields and joyous song. At the climax, the principal theme of the march was brought in fortissimo to accompany the immense cheering of the crowd.

Once during the performance, Grieg found his worst fears justified. The actor who sang the Song of the Kings was a good actor but not a good singer. Grieg, feeling sorry both for the efforts of the singer and for the slaughter of his music, sank lower and lower in his seat. Björnson, noticing him, whispered sternly, "Grieg! For heaven's sake, sit up properly!"

At the end of the performance, the audience was wild with delight. They called Grieg and Björnson many times to the stage. After the show, the composer went with his friend to Björnson's home to eat cheese in the kitchen and to laugh merrily over some of the comic mistakes made by the actor-singers.

Björnson's children came rushing in. "Just think!" they shouted to their smiling mother. "We were up in the gallery and saw Father and Grieg come on the stage!"

"We are a success!" boomed Björnson. "Our public from the gallery says so! A toast, Herr Grieg, a toast!"

Raising his wine-glass high, Grieg cried merrily: "Skål! To the Northland, skål!" Even in jest Grieg did not forget his purpose in composition—to express the spirit of northernism so that all the world would be enriched by new melodies and rhythms from the Viking past.

Björnson furnished the poetic basis for many other compositions besides *Sigurd Jorsalfar. At the Cloister Gate,* Opus 20, was one of these. The text—a scene from Björnson's drama, *Arnljot Gelline*—is a dialogue between a nun and a girl who knocks for admission at the gate of the convent late at night. With the question "Who's knocking so late at the cloister door?" the main theme is sounded. The girl's answer, "Homeless maiden from far away," has a musical setting sweet and pathetic. It is descriptive music of the sort Grieg knew so well how to write.

Landsighting, Opus 31, is fresh, robust music, depicting the landing of Olaf Trygvason from the ship which brought him across the North Sea from England. All the fire and hearty good humor of the huge and handsome Viking are in this music, which is designed for male chorus, baritone solo, and orchestra. Like many of the compositions dating from the Christiania years, *Landsighting* was written to order. It was performed at a bazaar to raise funds for the restoration of Trondhjem Cathedral.

Bergliot, a deeply moving melodrama by Björnson, was provided with a musical setting to which the heroic poetry was declaimed. The story was taken from the famous old *Harald Hadradis Saga,* where it is written that when Bergliot, wife of Einar Thambarskelvir who had led his men out to fight Harald Hadradi, heard that both her husband and her son Eindride had fallen in battle, she left the inn of Trondhjem and went at once to the castle. At the castle she found the peasant army gathered. Bergliot appeared before them, demanding that they march against the victorious Harald. The peasants, however, had come to the realization that a war between kings is no affair of the common people. While they delayed, King Harald came rowing down the river. Bergliot, realizing that all was lost, cried despairingly, "Now we miss here my cousin Hakon Ivarson. Einar's slayer would not row down the river if Hakon stood here on the bank."

In the brief prelude, Grieg's music shows us the emotions of Bergliot, anxiously waiting at the inn for news of the battle. Anxiety, foreboding, tenderness, anger, sorrow—all are blended in this splendid tone poem.

With what turbulence the music accompanies the words, "How the sand drifts down the road, and a clamor rises!" With what bleak longing does it paint the scene: "The open fjord and the low-lying hills; I remember the town of my childhood." How the music rises to a wrathful sonority when Bergliot makes the desperate effort to get the peasants to fight: "Up, up, peasants! He is fallen; but he who struck him down lives on! Shoot out, ye dragon-ships! Shoot out from the land! Vengeance on Harald!"

The most important part of the work musically is the funeral march at the end. Deep sorrow for a valiant hero changes to a pæan of praise and triumph. Throughout the march, we are reminded of Bergliot's soul-shaking, tearless sorrow. The grand music fades and dies as the procession passes by with a creaking of wagon wheels and finally disappears.

Of the music for Björnson's songs, the most appealing and characteristic is that for *The Princess*, in *Four Songs*, Opus 21. Here is an example of how Grieg could conjure up a picture of the far away and long ago with his odd choice of harmonies for his plaintive melodies. Björnson's words are wistful:

> "The princess is sitting alone in her bower.
>   The boy in the valley is piping his lay.
> Be still! for thy music doth fetter the thoughts
>   That fain would be wandering far, far away,
>   As the sun goes down,
>   As the sun goes down."

Grieg's music for this poem fades as majestically as the sunset colors.*

The success of their collaboration in producing *Sigurd Jorsalfar* and *Bergliot* convinced both Björnson and Grieg that they should write an opera together, Björnson to furnish the libretto, Grieg the music. Björnson had written *Arnljot* as the text for an opera, but Grieg got only so far as to "smell at it" as he put it.

"Why not write something about Olaf Trygvason?"

* See Appendix, page 249.

suggested Grieg one evening. He and Nina and the Björnsons were dining at a little restaurant where fine wines and cheese and Edvard's favorite Norwegian snow-hen were served. "To me there is no more colorful hero in all Norse history than that fearless warrior, half-civilized, half-barbarian. And his time, his age—men worshiping their old gods in temples sacred to Thor and Frey and Odin and Balder, believing in giants and kobolds and tolls."

"Are we Norwegians any different now?" laughed Björnson. "Don't we all believe in the folk under the hills and the water spirits with green hair and green teeth under the waterfall?"

"Exactly. We do halfway believe the old tales. And that is just why the subject of Olaf Trygvason in mighty combat with those who clung to the old faith in heathen gods will be attractive."

"It shall be done. To Trygvason!" Björnson raised his glass. "To Olaf Trygvason, fierce and mighty! He dared strike down the idols in their own temples, just as you are striking down the food and railway interests, Herr Grieg! He raised his mighty sword against ignorance and superstition!"

"Wait, wait!" laughed Nina. "Is this opera to be about Edvard or about Olaf Trygvason?"

It was not until the summer of 1873, however, that Grieg received the first three scenes of the opera. He and Nina were again in Bergen, though not at Landås this time. The beautiful estate had been sold, of necessity; for the elder Grieg had suffered severe financial losses.

It was a disappointment not to find the cozy little work-room waiting for him, thought Grieg with a secret sigh. His problem was soon settled, however. The wealthy Bergen brewer, Rolfsen, offered the composer a little summer house in the suburb Sandviken. There Grieg set to work to study the poem *Olaf Trygvason*.

The venture was ill-fated. After making a beginning with the music, Grieg wrote to ask Björnson for the remaining parts. Björnson delayed, and Grieg fretted. Then one day there came a letter from Henrik Ibsen. Ibsen proposed that his play *Peer Gynt* be set to music, and asked Grieg to undertake the work. Without consulting Björnson, Grieg agreed to make a start with *Peer Gynt*.

Björnson, hearing of the new plan, was deeply hurt, particularly since he imagined that *Peer Gynt* would be an opera. Grieg tried to explain that his music would be background music only and need not interfere with the plans for the opera. The misunderstanding, however, could not be easily explained away, and coolness took the place of the former warm friendship between Björnson and Grieg. Björnson blamed Grieg for failure to go on with their plans; Grieg placed the blame on Björnson's dallying. It is hard to say which was at fault; but the failure of this collaboration left the projected opera a mere fragment, published in 1889 as Opus 50.

The opening scene of *Olaf Trygvason* shows us the interior of an ancient Norse temple. The Vikings are celebrating their pagan rites, with invocations to the gods, sacrifices on the altar, and a weird dance in which the women are swung over the altar fires. Grieg caught the color of the period in his music. He transports us to the tenth century by subtle use of the old modes—the Lydian (the mode with intervals the same as those of the white keys of the piano between F and F); the Mixo-Lydian (intervals between G and G); the Phrygian (intervals between E and E); and the Dorian (intervals between D and D).

There are a chorus of worshipers, a sacrificial priest, a woman, and the Volva (wise woman) in the scene. The priest invokes the gods in a somber recitative. A gentle solo by the woman follows. The chorus chants, "Hear us! Hear us!" Suddenly the chorus breaks forth with "Other gods have come! Strong gods, victorious gods!" The music has a wild, barbaric joy in it as the scene closes.

In the second scene, the Volva conjures the good will of the gods with her chanting and incantations. Her voice is full of hate as she shrieks: "He is an evil man, he who comes from the South!" The gods give a sign that they will meet this Christian stranger who is coming from the South, this Olaf Trygvason. They will meet him in the temple and see who is the stronger. The chorus, incited by the Volva, is carried away by a frenzy of hate.

The final scene is a ceremonial scene—sacred games and dances around the sacrificial fire. Grieg's music provides a spirited round dance and a wild sword dance. The scene ends with the music in a whirling presto.

In this fragment, Grieg shows his mastery of the orchestra. There is an effective part at the beginning where the theme in the basses is written over the sustained note in the horns and the tremolo of the strings. There is vigor and fire in the music of the horn quartet supporting the baritone solo: "Now the drinking horn is raised, the horn of Odin, father of armies." Nothing could better define the fantastic rage of the Volva during her incantation than the shrill piccolo which accompanies her voice.

All the barbaric color, the dark fears of the ancient pagan age, the weird ceremony, and the savage dance rhythms are suggested by Grieg's music. *Olaf Trygvason* is the very essence of Norwegianism in music.

Both Grieg and Björnson tried to patch up their differences and finish the work in later years. But some warmth had gone forever from their friendship, even though they were both big enough eventually to shake hands and laugh at their childishness. Björnson might have been pronouncing an epitaph over the buried dreams for an opera when he said, years later, "What does not come at the right time never comes."

Wagner Theatre
Bayreuth

Chapter Sixteen

In sweet music is such art,
Killing care and grief of heart
Fall asleep, or hearing, die.

HENRY VIII

*I*N 1873, Grieg's friend Johan Svendsen, the Norwegian violinist and composer, returned to his native city
of Christiania from a long residence in France. Enemies
of the two great musicians immediately set to work to
bear tales, to whisper unkind remarks, and to create trouble between the two in every malicious way known to
jealous artists. All such plans came to nothing, however.
Grieg, in a letter of some years later, described his feeling toward Svendsen:

"All the more I am drawn to Svendsen's art, though
nothing could be more different than our artistic natural
endowments. He has taught me to believe in myself and
in the power and authority of the individual. There was

172

a time in Christiania when to be individual was the same as to be a criminal. But then Svendsen came and he was individual, and so the miracle happened that from then on I too was tolerated. There are few artists, therefore, to whom I owe more than to Svendsen."

All his life, Grieg, who fought every sort of ignorance and malice unrelentingly, displayed no jealousy toward rival artists. In this attitude toward his fellow musicians he exhibited that rare greatness of character which can acknowledge the worth of a competitor. In his music he could never have achieved the honesty and clarity that were his if he had not possessed fine qualities as a man; for, more than other artists, Grieg was his music, and his music was Grieg himself.

On June 1, 1874, the Norwegian government made grants to both Svendsen and Grieg—composers' honorariums. The yearly payment was enough to provide the economic security which Grieg needed.

A little dazed at the good news, Grieg turned to Nina. "We are free at last, my dear. Free to wander wherever we will, to live as we like, to compose—"

"No more teaching for you, Edvard," Nina said softly.

"And we can go back now to the beautiful Westland—leave this cold eastern country of ice and blizzards."

"And go back to Bergen's showers," teased Nina.

"I love every drop of rain that falls from Bergen skies. And you will, too, Nina. We shall find a comfortable place to live—'way up in some fjord, perhaps—and I shall write and write and write!"

Grieg made preparations to leave very soon after receiving the grant. He scurried around telling his friends goodbye—the Björnsons and the Beyers, the pleasant young couple who sang in the choir at the Philharmonic, his pupils, and some of the musicians of the Academy and Philharmonic. Svendsen was making plans to leave, too— to enter into the musical life of Denmark. For neither of these famous musicians was there much regret in seeing Christiania fade from view, Christiania which left its mark on every artist who ever lived there, the prosperous, cold city that had little time for art.

Nina and Edvard went immediately to Bergen, and the composer set to work in the pavilion in Sandviken. Ibsen's play *Peer Gynt* had taken possession of him in a disturbing way. He thought of it night and day. Its wild scenes and crude peasant characters, its almost barbarous hero and his fantastic adventures, its strange mixing of fact with fancy, and of sane everyday events with fairy tales and fairy-tale creatures—all these features of the play fascinated the composer.

"This is a folk play which only a Norwegian can appreciate fully," he would say, looking up suddenly from his plate at the dinner table; and Mother Grieg and Nina would scold him for bringing his work home with him.

For two years the music for *Peer Gynt* occupied almost all of Grieg's time. He struggled to compose the right background for Ibsen's play as he had never struggled before. He rewrote and discarded and changed again and again the scoring of the parts, sometimes despairing

of ever getting it down to his satisfaction. To his friend
Frants Beyer he wrote:

"*Peer Gynt* goes very slowly, and there is no possibility
of its being finished by autumn. It is a frightfully in-
tractable subject, with the exception of one or two parts,
as for example where Solvejg sings—all of which I have
done."

The music was not finished by fall. With the unfin-
ished music sheets in his trunk, Grieg packed off to Denmark in September. At New Year's he and Nina made
their way to Leipzig. By May they were back in Denmark,
to spend the summer with August Winding at Fredens-
borg. In the autumn they came home to Bergen. And all
the while the *Peer Gynt* music would give Grieg no peace,
and would not write itself.

In the autumn of 1875, Grieg's world seemed to come
crashing down around his head. In September his father
died, and his mother the following month. Not even
Alexandra's death had shocked Grieg as the loss of his
parents did. Life without the jolly, generous father and
the talented, understanding mother seemed unthinkable.
Grieg's gay spirits faltered, and many a cold rainy day
found him, all unmindful of soaked shoes and drenched
clothing, walking, walking beside the sea or climbing the
wind-lashed headlands.

Nina sighed to see him, crushed, borne down by a sorrow which she could not soften for him. A new look
came into the composer's eyes—a look half-questioning,
half-complaining. This expression was noted by many

great artists in later years, including the Russian composer
Tchaikovsky and the French critic Ernest Closson. Closson
once described this odd expression in Grieg's serious blue
eyes:

"His gaze is serious, wonderfully soft, with a peculiar
expression, at once worn, tentative, and childishly naïve.
The entire effect is of kindness, gentleness, candor, a
sincere modesty."

The composer and his wife moved in from Sandviken
to Grieg's boyhood home in Strandgaten, where they
lived with Brother John and his family through the winter. Grieg rented a workroom in town, and there he threw
himself feverishly into his work. It is typical of him that
he turned in this time of sorrow to Norwegian folk music,
pouring his grief into one of his greatest compositions,
the *Ballade* in G minor, Opus 24.

The *Ballade,* which is probably Grieg's best work for
piano solo, was built on a folk song from Valdes. Ingrid
the maid may have sung this old song when he was a boy,
and who knows what bitter-sweet memories it may have
brought to mind of the happy days in Strandgaten, when
Grandfather Hagerup came to take him to the fishmarket,
when Mother Grieg knitted while she listened to her
youngest son practicing his scales, when bluff Father
Grieg returned with presents from his trips across the
channel to England and Scotland.

The text of the old song runs:

"Many a lightsome song I know
Of lands under the southern skies;

But never yet the sturdy song
Of what at our doorstep lies.

So I will try if I cannot sing
A song that will make folk see
How fine it is in that North Country
The South treats so scornfully."

Grieg's music for this song of the North Country presents the beautiful theme with plaintive, nostalgic feeling. The variations on the theme are like a kaleidoscopic view of fjords and fjelds, the valleys and the snow-capped mountains, the dances of the people, the skirling of the fiddles. The climax is a brilliant display of all the resources of the piano.

Brahms was a great admirer of the deeply thoughtful, introspective *Ballade,* and Walter Niemann, a famous critic of the nineteenth century, called it "the most perfect musical embodiment of Norway and the Norwegian people, of its agonized longing for light and sun, and at the same time the most perfect embodiment in music of Grieg the man." *

From the *Ballade* Grieg plunged into the writing of some of his most inspired songs—one group to words of Henrik Ibsen, *Five Songs,* Opus 25; the second group to words of John Paulsen, Opus 26.

The *Minstrel's Song* from Opus 25 tells the favorite Norse story of the river sprite teaching the magic art of song in return for the musician's soul. There is something at once tragic and triumphant in *A Swan* from this

* See Appendix, page 249.

same group. It is as if Grieg had set down in this song his own triumph over sorrow. The final measures are a stirring setting for the words:

"And, with its ringing,
His spirit passed on then;
He died while singing.
Was he only a swan then—a swan then?"

In *The First Primrose* from Opus 26, Grieg has again captured the joy of life. The clouds of winter and sorrow are past for him, and the sun comes again.

In the meantime, Grieg had completed the *Peer Gynt* music. The play with its musical setting was performed for the first time in 1876, in Christiania.

Grieg was not present at the first performance, for in the spring he left Norway to spend a vacation with Feddersen in Denmark. The two made a trip that summer to Bayreuth, to attend the Wagner festival. They were present at the first complete performance of *Der Ring des Nibelungen* in August. The performance took place in the theater which had been built for Wagner's exclusive use. Wagner's royal friend, Ludwig II, King of Bavaria, had intended to finance the construction of the festival playhouse, but his personal fortune proved unequal to the task, and most of the money for the venture was eventually raised by Wagner Societies in Europe and elsewhere.

Grieg sent home an amusing description of the town of

Bayreuth, which had donated the site for the unique theater, and drew a vivid picture of the motley crowd of people who came to the first Bayreuth festival. Part of his letter read:

"This place so swarms with musicians, poets, painters from all the corners of the earth that one stumbles over them wherever one goes. From the whole of Europe the best names are assembled—they have come streaming even from America. In the long run, the flood of artists would be unendurable. I do not stay in a hotel but in a private house and imagined that at home I could be by myself. But no, in corridors, on stairs one meets the famous. Next to me lives a renowned composer of opera, on the other side of the corridor a famous singer, below a famous court bandmaster, and above a celebrated critic. As I sit here I hear Wagner motives being hummed, sung, yodeled, and bellowed from the garden. I go to the window and see Valkyrs and Rhine daughters, gods and human beings, strolling about in the shady alleys."

Grieg's admiration of Wagner's music was tinged with something akin to awe. There was always a gentle deference, too, in the way he spoke of Wagner the man, and a trifle of fear, perhaps, such as modest Frey may be supposed to have felt in the presence of thundering Thor.

Grieg met Wagner at the rehearsal of the "Ring," though hardly at the invitation of the great German composer. Hans Richter, who was conducting the festival orchestra, had been instructed to allow no one to attend rehearsals; but when Grieg begged to be allowed to sit quietly among the musicians in the pit and watch Wagner direct the singers, Richter remarked slyly, "I couldn't help it if you came *without* permission, of course."

Grieg was eagerly waiting when, at the final rehearsal, Wagner—irritable, worried with a thousand details, nervous and pale from strain—thundered the signal to begin. Wagner had given instructions that Grieg and a few others who had been admitted were to sit in the dark and maintain absolute silence; for the King of Bavaria— the "mad Ludwig" whose mania was a morbid fear of strange people—was to be present to witness privately this performance of his composer-friend's masterpiece. When Grieg and the other visitors disregarded instructions (to the extent of standing when a slight noise informed them that Ludwig had arrived), Wagner came to the edge of his box and scolded them as only he could, sparing no one's feelings in his angry and nervous state.

Grieg refused to take offense at Wagner's rudeness, which could not dim for him the joy he found in the art of the genius of Bayreuth. At Leipzig the boy Edvard had sat entranced through fourteen performances of *Tannhäuser*. Of the "Ring," Grieg, the mature Norwegian composer, wrote home from Bayreuth: "This music drama is the work of a giant, equaled perhaps in the history of art only by Michael Angelo."

In September, when Grieg returned to spend one last winter in Christiania, he saw *Peer Gynt* performed. Twice during the performance he had to leave his place and show himself on the stage—once after *Solvejg's Song* and again at the end of the play.

It was a strange play that Grieg's eyes watched that

night—a play made up of the antics of giant trolls and witch women, of the grotesque pranks of mortal men and women. It was an ugly play and a beautiful play, often bitter with satire, sometimes made palatable with downright foolishness. In it the great north country's humor and indescribable melancholy were striving for expression in words and music.

The full score of Grieg's music for *Peer Gynt* was not published until after his death. He arranged two of the songs, however, and published them—*Solvejg's Song* and *Solvejg's Cradle Song*—as Opus 23. The most effective parts of the background music he arranged in the form of suites—*Peer Gynt Suite I,* Opus 46, and *Peer Gynt Suite II,* Opus 55. The play with full musical score has been accepted as a true Norwegian folk drama, and as such is often performed on national holidays in the theaters of Bergen and Oslo.

The musical prelude to the first act is called *At The Wedding.* The principal theme—bold and lusty—portrays Peer Gynt, an untamed peasant lad, glowing with youth, dangerous in his desire to make his personality felt in the world. There is a break. Then a prolonged note on the horn indicates that something important is to come. As the horn ceases to sound, the harp's mild chords carry the listener into a different world. Clarinet and oboe alternately, to the accompaniment of harp and strings, play the delicate melody that symbolizes the gentle Solvejg. The viola follows, playing a *halling* and a *springdans.* All the color and noise and excitement of a peasant wedding are called up, but above all the clamor rises the tender,

melancholy motive that belongs to Solvejg. The semi-
quavers of a short coda bring the curtain up on the scene
between Peer Gynt and his mother, Åse:

The scene takes place on a mountainside near the farm
of pathetic old Åse and her son Peer Gynt. Åse is scolding
the ragged and impudent Peer, who has been off for many
days hunting in the mountains. He cares not a jot for her
words, and puts her off with a fantastic tale of meeting a
gigantic buck deer in the mountains. This deer, he says,
caused him to fall from the lofty ridge of Gendin, a fall
which Åse well knows no mortal being could survive.

"Downward still and ever downward!" Peer tells his
half-believing mother. And she cries, "Heaven help us!"
Then, says Peer, there was a mighty splash. "Buck he
swam and dragged me after—so I got home." His mother
asks anxiously if he is hurt, suddenly realizes that she is
being fooled, and cries, "What a pack of lies! All that
nonsense you've been telling is the tale of Gudbrand
Glesne, which I heard back in my childhood!"

Suddenly Åse grows serious. She tells Peter that Ingrid,
the girl whom he could have married had he not dallied
so long, is being married to another this day. She reproaches Peer for his shiftlessness; and, as she talks, there
is revealed a pathetic story.

Her husband had been a prosperous farmer, but too
fond of drink. Everyone was welcome to eat of the best
and drink of the best at the elder Peer's farm, and everyone accepted the generous hospitality until there was little
left of his fortune. Then the elder Peer had evaded his
responsibility by the simple method of dying, leaving a

run-down farm and no money to his widow and son.

Unhappy and bewildered, Åse has tried to console herself and her son with the fairy tales and witch tales she
heard in her youth. Peer has believed them, and Åse herself has not always been sure what was reality and what
was fancy. In such an eerie and fanciful world, Peer has
grown to manhood. Scorning hard work, wasting his time
in day-dreaming, he has become the joke of the village.
People avoid him. Noticing this, Peer becomes arrogant,
fighting and brawling to attract attention to himself.

Peer pretends not to care about Ingrid's marriage, but
he decides to go to the village, just to watch the wedding
celebration. Åse protests; so he calmly puts her on the roof
of the mill house, which sits on the bank of a stream running through the Gynt farm. Neighbors find her nearly
out of her wits with fright.

One of the neighbors calls for help: "Eivind! Anders!
Hi! Come here!"

"What is it?"

"Peer Gynt has put his mother upon the mill-house
roof."

And so the poor soul is rescued while Peer goes his
impudent way to the wedding.

The wedding is gay with dancing and music. Peer
wants to dance with the girls, but they shove him away
with disgust. He becomes more and more angry. A beautiful little peasant lass arrives with her mother and
father and younger sister. She is Solvejg, a gentle and
trusting girl, and of those present she alone sees something in Peer to like. The memory of her kind eyes lingers

with the rude Peer as he goes blundering about the court-
yard seeking for Ingrid. Some demon possesses him as he
sees Ingrid, and under the very nose of the bridegroom he
carries off the bride.

The musical introduction to the second act is called
Abduction of the Bride and *Ingrid's Lament.** The introduction is in agitated, almost frantic rhythm, to indicate
the distress of the wedding guests. The *Lament* is an inspired elegy in a mood of hopeless resignation and deep
sorrow.

Peer carries the terrified Ingrid into the mountains.
There he leaves her in spite of her pitiful crying. He
realizes that he cannot go back to the village; because of
this kidnaping, he will be hunted like a wild deer. He
wanders about the mountains, trying to think what to do.
He meets some girls from a *saeter,* one of the summer
farmhouses in the high pastures. The girls circle round
Peer in a scene full of deviltry. The music indicates the
wild, abandoned nature of their dance, their gross, earthy,
witchlike laughter.

Peer finally decides to build a hut for himself, but
before he can set to work on it he meets the troll daughter
of the Dovre King. She appears to him as a beautiful
woman in green and lures him to her father's palace.
There she dances for him—a grotesque dance to the accompaniment of cow-bells.

Peer is commanded to marry the troll woman. When
he refuses, the trolls and goblins—imps with horrid faces
and long, scratching fingers—torment him. The troll king

* See Appendix, pages 249 and 250.

leers at him, and the troll princess smiles wickedly out of a face suddenly become hideous and old. Peer has given up all hope of his life when the bells of the village ring and the mountain palace comes tumbling down.

The music for the scene in the mountain king's palace* is grotesque, achieving a powerful effect by the use of one motive only. This motive begins in the basses and 'cellos. Then the bassoons take it up, the violins carry it pizzicato. The tempo increases as the whole orchestra takes up the theme. It rises to a frenzied climax, to crash suddenly as the church bells sound.

Peer makes his escape. He sets about building a hut in the forest. One fine day, Solvejg comes to him and says that she will marry him. Peer feels ashamed before her. All his deviltry, his laziness, his selfishness seem too apparent in contrast with Solvejg's calm and beautiful nature. Peer runs away, but Solvejg does not return to the village. She stays on in the hut, spinning and singing her plaintive little song, and waiting for Peer's return.

Peer goes home. There he finds his mother, worn out with anxiety and want, on her deathbed. In a scene as pathetic as it is grotesque, Peer tries to comfort the poor old soul by telling her fanciful tales—the same tales she told him when he was a little boy. Grieg's music for this scene—Åse's Death—has been called one of the most impressive and somber threnodies ever written.†

Peer then goes wandering all over the world. He becomes very rich and has many adventures. At one time he

* See Appendix, page 250.
† See Appendix, page 251.

is accepted by an Arab tribe as a prophet. But deceitful Peer cannot play that role for long, and he steals away in the night with the chieftain's daughter, Anitra, who has charmed him with her graceful dancing.

Grieg wrote two dances for this part of the play. The sensuous *Arab Dance** portrays the graceful movements of the girls who come to dance before the prophet. *Anitra's Dance,* delicate and airy, has an Oriental mystery about it.†

Anitra proves as wily as Peer. She steals his money and his horse and returns to the tents of her father, leaving Peer stranded. As he moves across the burning sands of the desert a vision, like a mirage, appears before him. He sees Solvejg, a fair and handsome middle-aged woman, spinning in the sunshine before the door of her cabin. A herd of goats is feeding near at hand, and the sough of the wind in the pines is like the falling of rain. Grieg's plaintive music makes an exquisite setting for this song:

> "The winter may wane and the springtime go by,
>   The springtime go by,
> The summer too may vanish, the year may die,
>   The year may die:
> But one day you'll return, that in truth I know,
>   In truth I know,
> And here I'll await you as I promised long ago,
>   I promised long ago.

* See Appendix, page 251.
† See Appendix, page 252.

Busily spinning, Solvejg hums the beautiful *allegretto.**

Peer makes his way to Egypt. Standing before the statue of Memnon at break of day, he hears it sing. Legend had it that the statue greeted the sunrise thus, but no one but foolish Peer believed the story. The strangeness and un-earthly quality of the statue's singing has been caught in Grieg's music called *Morning Mood.*†

Finally Peer returns to Norway. He is shipwrecked off the coast. The background music depicting the fury of the storm, the creaking of the ship's rigging, the cries of the drowning sailors, is a magnificent tone poem.‡

Peer is the only survivor of the wreck. He goes back to the forest near his old home and sets about the task of building a little hut. He finds no peace, however, for the trolls discover him and the ugly daughter of the Dovre King appears to torment him. He is pursued by imps and devilish apparitions called *thread-balls,* and at every cross-roads, he meets the sinister figure of the button-molder, who tells Peer that he must be put back in the big pot, melted down with other misfits, and molded all over again.

One day Peer wanders along a path that seems vaguely familiar. He comes in sight of the hut he had built long ago and which he abandoned when Solvejg came to him in the forest. Solvejg, old and silver-haired, stands in the doorway. Peer throws himself at her feet, asking forgive-ness for his selfish life and wicked deeds. Solvejg gently

* See Appendix, page 253.
† See Appendix, page 254.
‡ See Appendix, page 254.

cradles his weary head in her arms. As the sun rises she sings the beautiful melody known as *Solvejg's Cradle Song.*

Christiania was as cold as usual, both as to weather and as to artistic efforts. In December, the Griegs left never to return, except for short concert engagements. In order to "earn some cash," as Grieg put it, he and his wife went to Upsala and Stockholm in Sweden, where they gave concerts. By summer they had decided to go to the beautiful Hardanger Fjord, to take rooms with some peasant family on a little secluded farm. This was a momentous decision for Grieg. Hardanger offered a veritable treasure house of nature impressions and folk ways. At Hardanger, the composer wrote some of his most charming tone poems.

Chapter Seventeen

Here shall he see
No enemy
But winter and rough weather.
AS YOU LIKE IT

ABOUT St. John's Day in 1877, Grieg and Nina settled at upper Börve in Ullensvang, which is on the Hardanger Fjord. They chose for their summer home a farm on a steep hillside overlooking the Sörfjord.

"Here I shall be able to compose," declared Grieg as he and Nina explored their new surroundings. "Look, Nina, did you ever see anything more magnificent?" He was pointing to the Fogelfonn glacier on the great mountain overlooking the fjord. Cool green where the shadows lay and frosty white in the sunshine, the glacier spread its chill mantle over the lofty cliffs. From a ravine higher up the fjord a fast-rushing river plunged in a thunderous

189

fall over mossy boulders to the sea-water of the fjord.

"I hope all this will help you. You are not at all well these days." Nina folded around her husband's shoulders a light shawl she had brought along.

"Nina, you fuss over me like a hen with one chick," declared Edvard, smiling at her over the folds of the old-fashioned shawl. Nevertheless, he left the wrap in place and was secretly glad of its warmth. He was suffering more and more with the passing years from asthma.

His failing health had a decided effect on his composing. He found it difficult to sit long hours at piano and work table. He was forced to put his musical thought into short forms—songs and short lyrical pieces for piano.

Five minutes' walk from the farmhouse at Börve was a little schoolhouse, empty during the summer months. Grieg got permission to use this school for a studio; like the workroom at Landås and the gardener's hut at Sölleröd, the school offered Grieg the quiet and freedom from interruption he required when he composed.

Writing to the poet John Paulsen, Grieg spoke of his workroom: "It is a lovely Sunday morning. I am sitting in the schoolhouse in which I have commandeered a workroom and can see the churchgoers rowing past out on the Sörfjord. They are making for Ullensvang. Meantime, I shall go into another church, the great church of memory, and let my thoughts rise up like pillars towards beauty and light."

During that summer he made use of the Lindeman collection again. Using twelve of the folk melodies as a base, he composed an *Album of Part Songs,* for men's voices,

Opus 30. There are some amusing songs in this group, particularly among the nursery songs. The *Lullaby,* where one voice makes the sound of a cat mewing all through the song, is as bright and gay as the Norwegian meadows in summer.

Grieg was delighted with the customs and the manners of the peasants of Hardanger. On his walks during the long days and light evenings, he visited many neat little farms along the fjord. The never-failing "Welcome, Herr Grieg," delighted him. He would sit at the scrubbed pine table in some cozy kitchen, listening to the tales the old grandmother of the household had to tell, delighting in her vigorous folk expressions and salty humor. He took the sturdy blond children on his knee while he and they listened to the peasant father play a tune on the harding-fele. He lent a hand at the churning, and got the dairy-maids to sing for him the odd songs of their fjord region. And at Börve, Nina and the good housewife of the farm prepared many a dinner or *middag* for the neighbors, who came gaily dressed in their traditional costumes for "Herr Grieg's pleasure" and stayed to eat heartily of rye bread, cheese, snow-hen, and fish, and to drink heartily of Hardanger ale.

When winter came, Grieg decided that Börve was too isolated a spot. He and Nina chose the neighboring town of Lofthus, where they lived with the Utne family. Hans Utne and his wife, Brita, completely won the hearts of the Griegs. Their hospitality, sensitive appreciation of Grieg's work and their admiration of Nina's singing, their understanding of the needs of the little couple never failed. They became the lifelong friends of Edvard and Nina. In later years, when concert tours took Grieg all over Europe, he was never too busy to find a moment to sit down to write a letter to his peasant friends at Lofthus.

William Peters, the painter, lived at Lofthus that year. He and Grieg spent many happy days together, rowing about the fjord, fishing, walking along the country roads, climbing the winding sheep paths in the hills. A charming description of Grieg at work in the little hut which had been constructed for him by Hans Utne was written by Mr. Peters many years later.

There was no road to the hut, which had been placed in an isolated spot. Grieg found it next to impossible to compose while anyone, even Nina, listened. The hut was but a square box, large enough for a fireplace, a piano, and Grieg. Peters wrote:

"Grieg could see, like Odin from Lidskjalf, whenever anybody tried to approach from afar."

On rainy days Grieg and Peters went fishing. Peters wrote: "We would put on our fishing togs and sit for hours in a small boat, hauling in fish while the mist made fantastic caps and hoods for the mountain peaks, and a musical quiet reigned undisturbed except for the jovial song of a bird or two, while the faraway waterfalls furnished the tuneful undertone."

Peters described also the stormy days in winter, "when the wind shook our house, rattling doors and windows like spirits playing an immense orchestra. Grieg sat in a corner listening." And as to Grieg's work methods, Peters said: "I have known composers who, in writing a little song, would use up a cartload of paper. Not so with Grieg. He would use only a single sheet! He wrote his music with a lead pencil, rubbed out, and substituted, and changed again, until he was satisfied. Then he wrote it over in ink, and sent to the publisher the same sheet with which he began."

Curious people soon found their way to Grieg's work hut, and this he could not tolerate. It was decided that the little house should be moved, "in the American way." It was hardly American, however, the method employed to move that hut to a more secluded spot. All of Grieg's peasant neighbors volunteered to come on "moving day." They appeared with ropes, logs, hooks, spades, shovels— in short, every tool they could lay hands on to help move the little "Piano Box."

Grieg had made preparations of his own for the day. He had provided stacks of the thin oatcakes called *flatbrödlefser* and jars full of sweet biscuit known as *kringler*. There were barrels of Hardanger ale, too, for those who grew thirsty from their efforts. The hearty farm men literally picked the little building from its foundation, placed it on logs, and with ropes drew the logs over the uneven, rocky soil to a spot overlooking the fjord. There they set the hut down, behind a screen of trees and bushes, on a cliff so sheer that no boat could tie up there. Hidden from the road and inaccessible to swimmers and rowers, Grieg felt that he would have privacy at last.

After the moving of workroom and piano, Grieg

played for his friends—hallings and springars and gang-ars—and the jovial crowd danced on the open space beside the hut. Long tables had been spread with food. Nina and Brita Utne helped serve the food, and Grieg himself passed the ale. The dancing grew merrier and merrier, the laughter rang out lustily. At the height of the merriment, Grieg and Nina slipped quietly away, smiling at the thought of their friends who had taken a whole day off from their own work to move the workroom at Lofthus in "the American way."

In this hut at Lofthus, Grieg completed an important work—the String Quartet in G minor, Opus 27.* In this work Grieg broke completely with the traditional quartet form, abandoning the polyphonic style to make use of a strict melodic-harmonic technique. In the String Quartet Grieg was definitely writing music of the future. Ten years later, Debussy sought support from Grieg's break with tradition in writing his own quartet. Grieg knew very well what he was doing when he composed this work. Writing to Matthison-Hansen, he said:

"I have lately completed a string quartet which, how-ever, I have not heard yet. It is in G minor and is not planned to be meat for small minds! It aims at breadth, vigor, flight of imagination, and, above all, fullness of tone for the instruments for which it is written."

Four Album Leaves for piano, Opus 28, were prepared for publication. The fourth only was written at Lofthus; the middle part of this piece was inspired by some music Grieg heard the peasant fiddlers playing as they rowed

* See Appendix, page 255.

past his work hut. The *Dance Caprice* from Opus 28 is
Grieg in gay and festive mood.*

Improvisation on Two Norwegian Folk Songs, for
piano, Opus 29, was written to order. It was a gift from
Grieg to help pay for the Holberg monument in Bergen.

The third work completed at Lofthus was *Taken into
the Mountains,* for baritone solo, string orchestra, and two
horns. The text was a verse from Landstad's *Norwegian
Folk Songs.* The passionate intensity and power of this
work have seldom been equaled. Grieg's letter to a friend
indicated how much it had cost him to write the music:
"This piece," he wrote, "contains drops of my heart's
blood."

> "I have been where the troll lives,
> The troll ran after me . . ."

Thus the great vocal work begins. The music has a bleak
Northern tinge. A sigh runs through it, as if all the people
in the dark valleys and on lonely farms in the snowdrifted
mountains were crying out for the summer sun. There is
more in it, too. It is the artist crying out for the sun of
recognition. Dark clouds of despair cover him; want and
cold and hunger are his daily companions. He dwells on
the cold heights, he descends into the dark valleys, he
longs for the sun.

The fall of 1878 found the Griegs making a concert
tour. At Cologne and Leipzig Grieg gave several concerts.
The German critics with all the malice at their disposal
tore his compositions to bits.

* See Appendix, page 256.

Grieg's warm admirer, the famous German pianist and composer Johannes Brahms, heard rumors of the cold reception which the Norwegian composer's music had received in Leipzig, and was inclined to see ironic humor in the situation. To his friend Elisabet von Herzogenberg Brahms wrote (Vienna, December 15, 1878): "Grieg was in Leipzig, too. How did he get on? I read a bad account of him in Rieter's paper just now—which looks hopeful!"

Brahms' admiration was based on a careful study of Grieg's work. His own compositions (notably the D-minor *vivace* which closes the andante in F major of the second violin sonata, Opus 100) began to show the influence of his illustrious Norwegian contemporary. Heinrich Herzogenberg chided Brahms playfully on the Norwegian coloring of the *vivace* in a letter dated 1887: "The Andante from the violin sonata! We fell in love with it on the spot, of course. At first I did not quite like the idea of the lovely F-major lady's betrothal to that melancholy Norwegian jester: however—so long as the union turns out well and they have plenty of children!"

Bitterly Grieg shook his head over the hostile and often malicious comments in the German press. The lonely artist, longing for the sun, turned his face toward home. He gave a concert in Copenhagen. One more concert followed, in Leipzig. The warm applause of the audience was Grieg's answer to the German critics. In the summer he was again in Lofthus.

On his birthday, friends came to celebrate with him. He was overjoyed when Ole Bull appeared with the young American girl who had married him after the death of Bull's first wife. Mrs. Bull preserved in writing her memory of that day:

"The little study of one room erected by the composer for perfect retirement was perched halfway up a rock and near the fjord. In the field above, the apple trees were in bloom about an old farmhouse, where the guests assembled. From the summit of the beetling cliffs not far away fell a beautiful waterfall, while the opposite mountain shore of the broad fjord, clothed with heavy forests of pine above and the feathery birch below, presented range after range of lofty peaks and domes crowned by the great Fogelfond with its eternal snow. The day was as perfect as friendship, music, and lovely surroundings could make it."

Chapter Eighteen

ALMOST before he realized it, Grieg was a world-famous figure. Letters from all the capitals of Europe offered him profitable engagements as conductor and concert pianist. Grieg accepted many of these offers, in spite of the hacking cough and his growing difficulty with breathing. The fact was, he found it increasingly difficult to compose.

"I am afraid Pegasus is good only to the very young and the very robust," he would complain to Nina.

When ideas did not come he worried himself sick, fearing that his creative powers were failing. The offers to go on tour were a release from his nervousness and worry. They filled the barren weeks between fits of inspiration.

The years 1878 to 1880 were years of almost constant travel. But Grieg somehow managed to get home to Bergen and Lofthus for the summer months. It was during the summer of 1880 that the urge to write music came to him after an uncreative period of two years. The inspiration for his work this time was a book of poems by A. O. Vinje. With the Vinje poems as a base, Grieg wrote his *Twelve Melodies to Poems of A. O. Vinje,* Opus 33. This collection contains some of Grieg's most inspired songs.

In *Springtide* the poet expresses the feelings of one who, knowing that his days are limited, is viewing the last spring he expects to see.

> "Now once again have I seen spring at hand,
>   And winter a vagrant,
> Hedges and trees by the south wind are fann'd,
>   Their blossoms all fragrant."

Grieg's music expresses the regret and longing of this poem perfectly.*

When the great Russian composer Tchaikovsky heard Nina Grieg sing this song in Leipzig, he was so deeply impressed that he wept. To express his admiration, he sent Nina a copy of his own songs with a cordial dedication.

Springtide and *Wounded* from Opus 33 were transcribed by the composer for string orchestra, and—published as *Two Elegiac Melodies,* Opus 34, with their titles

* See Appendix, page 256.

changed to *The Last Spring* and *Heart Wounds*—soon became known the world over.

On the Journey Home from the Vinje songs expressed Grieg's own feelings when he was on tour. It is the longing of a traveler to far places for the familiar scenes of home.

> "My childhood speech I hear about me saying
> The words that make my heart with sweet grief glow,
> With such keen recollections is it blended
> I scarce can walk as my lone way is wended."

Grieg, far from home, yearned for the familiar sights of home, for the speech of the market place. All this he has written into the music for *On the Journey Home.**

The Old Mother was composed with Grieg's own mother in mind.

> "Dear mother, thou art old and poor,
> Hast toiled so hard and long,
> But still thy loving heart is warm,
> Thou gavest me this sturdy arm
> And all my courage strong."

The music is both sad and heroic—courage triumphing over life itself.†

In August 1880, Grieg accepted the post of conductor of the Bergen Harmonic Society. This was a gesture of good will on his part, for he well knew that there would be little artistic satisfaction in the task of whipping a

* See Appendix, page 256.
† See Appendix, page 257.

rather poor orchestra into shape and instructing an amateur choir.

The same August that Grieg accepted the directorship of the home-town Harmonium, Ole Bull returned from his last tour of America. He was not the same Ole Bull, but an old man, pale with fatigue and illness. Grieg visited him on the isle of Lysöen, where the violinist had built a magnificent home after moving from Österöen. Ole Bull lay in his bed, watching through his bedroom windows the sea birds and the clouds like lamb's fleece in the sky. The room was sweet with heather from the hills.

"My last summer, Grieg. My last summer," he sighed.

During the depressing days when Ole Bull lay sick to death in his island home Grieg found little consolation in work with the amateurish musicians of Bergen's Harmonium. In order to shape a presentable program for the first concert of the season, the composer was forced to call often at the homes of the performers, to instruct them in some part of their playing with which they were having difficulty—a matter of teaching, pure and simple.

On August 17, 1881, Ole Bull died. All the steamers in the harbor of Bergen went out to meet the little craft that brought his body from the "isle of light" to the mainland. At his funeral on August 23, Björnson and Grieg walked in the procession, Grieg carrying the gold laurel wreath that had been given to Ole Bull in San Francisco. And at the first Harmonium concert, Grieg opened the program with *Saeter Girl's Sunday* in memory of genial Ole Bull, who had understood and loved Norway well. With this melancholy beginning Grieg assumed in earnest the duties which were to task both his strength and his patience greatly.

In 1881, Grieg wrote to Matthison-Hansen: "I am conducting the Harmonic concerts and am fretting myself sick over it." When he gave up the job at the end of two years, he wrote: "My players, especially the winds, were simply awful, and after two years I could stand it no longer. Yet I wished you could have heard our phrasing in Schubert's C major symphony and Handel's anthems. I really made something of the choir. But, of course, I came into collision with the directors, who either could not or would not understand me, and I waded in trouble, anonymous mud-slinging, and all that goes with that sort of thing." Never again did Grieg accept an appointment that would keep him tied to one spot.

During these difficult months in Bergen he turned to folk sources for the necessary stimulation of his creative talents. In Lindeman's *Mountain Melodies* he found the inspiration for the duets for piano, Opus 35: *Four Norwegian Dances*. The *Halling from Amot* is a characteristic Norwegian peasant dance from this collection.* The delightful grace with which Grieg always rendered the first movement of the *Halling* has been remembered by all who heard him play it.

With the passing years, Grieg grew more and more restless, giving concerts, making brief flitting journeys home to Norway during the summers. Even at Bergen and in Hardanger he was not willing to remain still for

* See Appendix, page 258.

long. With the musician-friends from Denmark and his good friend Frants Beyer, who had come to live on the west coast of Norway, he traveled almost every year into the mountains of the Jotunheim, making long walking tours in spite of his asthma and gradually failing lung. All this moving about was in reality a substitute for composition. In 1883 Grieg wrote to Dr. Abraham in Leipzig: "And now for a word about Pegasus. He has certainly been here, but 'presto' I could not exactly call him—nor could I call him 'allegro'; if I were to christen him his name would have to be 'andante, quasi lento'."

Grieg tried another piano concerto, but gave it up. He turned more and more to the shorter forms when the mood to compose was upon him.

In 1883 he wrote a sonata for violoncello and piano in A minor. His skillful use of the 'cello here is no doubt due to the helpful suggestions of his brother John, who played the instrument well and knew its requirements. The sonata, published as Opus 36, was dedicated to John.

The *tranquillo* second subject of the first movement gives the piano a quiet, flowing melody, and the 'cello, as a middle voice, is used effectively.*

In the finale, the 'cello carries a sprightly little tune,* and the same tune becomes a wistful second subject, truly Norse in coloring.*

Two Waltz-Caprices for piano, Opus 37, and *Lyrical Piece* for piano, Opus 38, date from this same year of 1883. The waltzes are graceful little compositions in the Viennese style. In the *Lyrical Pieces* Grieg was at his best,

* See Appendix, page 258.

as usual, with Norwegian subjects. The *Berceuse* is a truly Norwegian cradle song, robust, mettlesome, with the cross-rhythm—two notes against three—so characteristic of Norse folk music. It is a lullaby for a peasant baby rocked in a crude cradle in some remote farmhouse.*

The compositions of 1883 exhausted Grieg's creative mood once more, and he was off to tour the capitals of Europe again. Dresden, Leipzig, Meiningen, Breslau, Frankfurt, Carlsruhe, The Hague, Rotterdam, Amsterdam, Rome—in rapid succession he played and conducted in all these cities. On the journey north from Rome he and Nina spent a few weeks on beautiful Lago Maggiore, one side of which touches the southern canton of Switzerland known as Tessin. The sight of lake and mountains made the composer long for the mountains and fjords of home, and in the beginning of June he was back in Bergen. By July he was boarding with the Utnes of Lofthus, forcing himself to take up his neglected composing.

Frants Beyer had built a home at Naesset on Nordasvannet, seven miles from Bergen. The Griegs went to visit him, and Grieg was immediately possessed with the idea of building a home of his own.

"A home is what we need, Nina," he declared. "All this running about does us no good. We could settle ourselves into a home, and I could compose as I used to. I know it!"

So Grieg bought a hill near Naesset and made plans immediately for building. The architect Schack Bull, who

* See Appendix, page 259.

was Grieg's cousin, was put in charge. By December 15, the first story of the house was completed.

"What shall we call it?" Nina wondered. "Every new home must have a name, you know, like a new baby."

"Let's call it *Troldhaugen*—Hill of the Trolls," suggested Grieg.

"You and your fairy tales," laughed Nina, but she, too, liked the sound of the name, and so the estate was christened.

While the home was a-building, Grieg set to work to write a cantata for the Holberg Jubilee. The work was performed on December 3, 1884, and was not particularly to Grieg's liking. Writing to his friend Julius Röntgen, he said:

"So far as music is concerned, I have had a wearisome time, as I have had to busy myself with a cantata for male voices a capella. This affair I have to conduct on December 3 (Holberg's 200th anniversary) on the market-place in Bergen, where the monument is to be unveiled. I can see it all before me: Snow, hail, storm, and every kind of foul weather, huge male chorus with open mouths, the rain streaming into them, myself conducting with waterproof cape, winter coat, galoshes, and umbrella! And a cold afterward, of course, or goodness knows what kind of illness! Oh well, it's one way of dying for one's country!"

Grieg did not provide this work with an opus number, but a very important work grew out of it: *From Holberg's Time*, for string orchestra, Opus 40. By the use of the old modes, Grieg gives an antique tone to the music. The

Prelude is sedate, with the elegance of the rococo period in its phrases. The Sarabande, an old dance, is quiet, almost elegiac. The Gavotte is gay, the Musette saucy. The Air* is simple and grave, like the song of a thoughtful minstrel playing for himself alone when the members of the court are away. The Rigaudon is sparkling and sunny.

In March, Grieg went up to Troldhaugen every day to watch the workmen put the finishing touches to his new home. In April he and Nina moved in. The dedication wreath was hung upon the door, and there was a house-warming to which came John and his family and the Beyers and many other friends of Bergen and the neighboring villages.

Late in the evening, Grieg motioned mysteriously to Frants Beyer. "Come, I want to show you something beautiful," he whispered. Leading Beyer up a narrow stairway, Grieg took him into the square tower which flanked one corner of the house. A door opening on the roof admitted them to an open-air platform, rail-enclosed. Grieg spread his arms to the star-studded sky. The distant plash of water and a faint stirring of wind like whispers in the pines were the only sounds in the quiet night.

"You have a regular observatory here, Grieg." Beyer spoke admiringly. "What a view! And what a place for observing our Northern Lights!"

"Ah, yes, but more than that. I shall feel myself close to Mother Nature here—the stars, the clouds, the pines shall be my companions, and from them I shall receive

* See Appendix, page 259.

the old inspiration." He spoke wistfully. Grieg the artist could not be content if he did not feel the urge to compose. The rest of his life was spent in the shadow of a depressing fear lest his genius was dying. That his fears were unfounded, that he would continue to write beautiful music almost to the day of his death Grieg did not suspect.

Chapter Nineteen

Beauty, truth, and rarity,
Grace in all simplicity.
THE PHOENIX AND THE TURTLE

$\mathcal{F}$RANTS BEYER lived on a little cove across from Troldhaugen, and he and Grieg used to visit each other by boat. Fishing and rowing about the fjord, they sometimes talked, sometimes remained silent, at all times respected each other's opinions and moods.

Beyer, who was a hearty, optimistic man, enjoyed playing a joke now and again on his absent-minded composer-friend. One day while they were drifting about lazily on the fjord, Grieg suddenly had an inspiration for a song. Taking a piece of paper from his pocket, he quickly jotted down a few notes. Then, in his careless way, he laid the paper beside him in the boat and proceeded to forget about it. The wind caught it up and would have swept it overboard had not Beyer—unnoticed—rescued it. He

208

studied the notes, slipped the paper into his pocket, and began to whistle the melody. Quick as a flash Grieg looked at him.

"Where did you get that melody?"

"Oh, it's just a little something I thought up just now!"

A look of wonder came into Grieg's eyes. "You don't say!" he said seriously, never doubting his friend's word. "Curious. I just thought of that melody myself."

Walking among the Iceland poppies, wild strawberries, and roses of his half-tame, half-wild garden, Grieg was seized with the old restlessness. He was off again in the fall, to give concerts in Christiania and Copenhagen. A transcription of six of his songs, for piano, Opus 41, and another book of *Lyrical Pieces,* Opus 43, were by this time off the press.

Opus 43 contains some of Grieg's best-known short works for the piano. In *Butterfly* he caught all the graceful fluttering movements, the dainty flight, and the gorgeous color of a butterfly dipping and rising above a bed of flowers.

In *Little Bird** he paints a happy picture of the coming of a bird in spring. *Erotik* is the embodiment of youthful longings awakened by the coming of the Northern spring. *To Spring*† embodies another emotion roused by the coming of spring; it is a picture of awakening nature against a background of a dark, bitter winter.

Home once more in July of 1886, he made with the poet Holger Drachmann a tour of the Jotunheim. For

* See Appendix, page 260.
† See Appendix, page 260.

Grieg, these walking tours were becoming more and more a necessary escape from his dark thoughts.

Drachmann wrote poetry inspired by the scenes of the high mountain region of Norway. Grieg set these poems to music. The songs thus composed were about the saeters where dairy-maids and lonely shepherds lived through the summer months, about the milking of cows and the making of butter and cheese. They were called *Four Songs from Fjeld and Fjord,* Opus 44.

The subjects of these songs are four young peasant girls whom the poet and composer met on the way: Johanna, Ragnhild, Ingeborg, and Ragna. While the saeter girls milked the cows and sang folk songs in the brisk morning air, Grieg would place a piece of paper on the broad back of the milk cow and jot down the milkmaid's songs—thus getting music "direct from the cow," as he put it.

These lyrics, written amid the scenes which inspired them, are not Grieg's best work. He had forgotten his own advice of a former year: "One must not go after nature impressions with the idea of creating at the time one receives the impression. For I have found that does not work." Grieg knew well that an artist must have time to digest his impressions mentally if they are to be invested with his own personality.

Grieg returned from the Jotunheim more determined than ever to write a long work. It was his habit to apologize for the short lyrical works. "I will fight my way through the great forms, cost what it may," he declared.

His determination brought results. During the winter of 1887-1888 he composed the Violin Sonata in C minor,

Opus 45. This is a mature work, somber, even tragic in tone, a work of breadth and power. Ernest Closson, the French critic, once said: "It must be classed with the most inspired scores ever written. . . . Had Grieg composed nothing but this sonata it would suffice to hand his name down to posterity." In December 1888, the work was performed in the Gewandhaus in Leipzig, with Adolf Brodsky playing the violin and Grieg himself at the piano.

Nearly twelve months before—on New Year's Day of that same year of 1888—an historic meeting had taken place at the home of Adolf Brodsky in Leipzig. At that meeting three of Europe's greatest composers sat down at table with the second greatest violinist of his time. The composers were the Norwegian Edvard Grieg, the German Johannes Brahms, and the Russian Peter Ilich Tchaikovsky; and the violinist (whose only superior was the great Joseph Joachim) was Brodsky, their host. In a letter to his brother, Tchaikovsky described the meeting:

"Next day I took a walk (it was New Year's Day), and went back to dine with Siloti* at Brodsky's. He was just trying a new trio by Brahms. The composer himself was at the piano. Brahms is a handsome man, rather short and stout. He was very friendly to me. Then we sat down to table. Brahms enjoys a good drink. Grieg, fascinating and sympathetic, was there too. In the evening I went to the Gewandhaus, when Joachim and Hausmann played the new Double Concerto of Brahms for violin and 'cello, and the composer himself conducted."

* Alexander Siloti, now living in New York City, a remarkable pianist. He was a friend of Tchaikovsky and later of Rachmaninoff, and was one of Liszt's most brilliant pupils.

Grieg and Tchaikovsky, meeting for the first time in the friendly home presided over by those "charming, really good Russian women" (as Tchaikovsky called them), Brodsky's wife and sister-in-law, were immediately attracted to each other. Tchaikovsky recorded the impression which Grieg made on him (in *Diary of My Tour in 1888*):

"There entered the room a very short, middle-aged man, exceedingly fragile in appearance with shoulders of unequal height, fair hair brushed back from his forehead, and a very slight, almost boyish, beard and moustache. There was nothing very striking about the features of this man, whose exterior at once attracted my sympathy, for it would be impossible to call them handsome or regular; but he had an uncommon charm, and blue eyes, not very large, but irresistibly fascinating, recalling the glance of a charming and candid child. I rejoiced in the depths of my heart when we were introduced to each other, and it turned out that this personality, which was so inexplicably sympathetic to me, belonged to a musician whose warmly emotional music had long ago won my heart. It was Edvard Grieg."

Again Grieg was roaming about Europe. After the winter in Leipzig, it was London, Berlin, and Paris that drew him like a magnet; in London he met with enormous success. For years he went again and again to the land across the channel, where both public and critics were warm in their praise, and where eventually he was honored with the *Doctor of Music* degree from both great universities—Cambridge (1894) and Oxford (1906).

No matter how far he traveled, however, Grieg was always home again on St. John's Day. Walking tours for his health, followed by weeks of dogged persistence at his composing, were his summer regimen.

In 1888 he produced another book of *Lyrical Pieces,* Opus 47. The next summer he wrote *Six Songs,* to words of German poems, Opus 48. *Six Songs* to words of Holger Drachmann, Opus 49, followed, and in the summer of 1891 an especially fine group of *Lyrical Pieces,* Opus 54, came from his workroom at Troldhaugen.

The *Gangar* from Opus 54 illustrates Grieg's use of secondary sevenths in daring sequence. *March of the Dwarfs* is an eerie piece of fantasy, striking in harmony and melody.* *Bell Ringing* is a curious reproduction on the piano keys of the clangor of bells.† Dissonances and strange harmonies suggest the brazen voices of big and little bells.

That summer of 1891 Grieg went with Röntgen and Beyer to the Jotunheim. At a tourist hut high in the mountains they met Gjendine Slålien, a beautiful Norwegian girl, who could sing the old songs and blow the great goat-horn. One evening Grieg heard her singing to her sister's baby, and it was the melody of her song that he used in his beautiful *Cradle Song,* Opus 66.

The goat-horn, which Gjendine sounded for them, produces only the first three notes of a minor scale. These three notes were the motive Grieg used to build his

* See Appendix, page 261.
† See Appendix, page 261.

Longing for Home, in *Lyrical Short Pieces,* Opus 57. This song is written in the old Lydian mode (the major scale with augmented fourths), which is the mode of the most characteristic of Norwegian dances.

With the coming of fall Grieg's restless feet took him away once more. This time he went to Christiania, where a torchlight procession of the students celebrated the twenty-fifth anniversary of Grieg's concert-giving in the eastern city. Grieg, watching the impressive ceremony in the still winter night, sighed contentedly. Life, after all, had been a success. Pegasus, sometimes weary, had not entirely deserted him.

"It is good," he murmured to himself. "Yes, life is good."

Grieg's name was known in every country of Europe. All the important capitals had paid him homage. On June 11, 1892, Norway proved to him that sometimes a prophet is honored even in his own country. That date marked Edvard's and Nina's silver wedding.

Morning had scarcely dawned when the presents began to appear. Wagons and carts and boys on bicycles brought gifts of flowers, stacks of messages from all over the world, pictures, a huge bearskin rug, silverware, even a Steinway piano from lovers of art in Bergen.

The Griegs entertained one hundred and thirty guests at a dinner in their garden. In the evening two hundred and thirty singers came out to serenade them. Grieg played the piano for the assembled people and Nina sang. The little couple, smiling and tired, were toasted again and again, and cannon thundered from the neighboring islands. Bengal lights and St. John's bonfires sprang up on every point as soon as darkness settled down, showing up the boats with holiday crowds who had rowed out to see the celebration.

"There, you see? In spite of all your troubles in Christiania and Bergen, you are loved and appreciated," Nina declared.

"These are the people, the everyday folks of Norway. My troubles have been with professional musicians and critics," Grieg reminded her.

"Well, as long as the common people love you, you are secure," said Nina firmly.

Grieg nodded. Thinking back over his life, his mind darted to event after event which proved her statement. No one had fought harder than Grieg in the struggle for Norwegian freedom from Sweden; no one had hated the government of the ruling nation more. Yet once when Grieg gave a concert in Sweden he was impressed by the friendliness of the people. Writing of that experience, he had said: "But this I tell you: That nothing will make me believe any more in hatred between peoples, for the people's wish is towards good understanding, that is the strong impression I received." Independently, he had arrived at the truth of the warning of Thomas Paine, the American revolutionary: "We must not confuse the peoples with their government."

Grieg turned more and more to nature for his inspiration. The years at Troldhaugen produced tone poems and songs formed on impressions of the Norwegian landscape. The *Five Songs* of Opus 60 include *A Bird Flew Scream-*

ing. The opening bars on the piano are a real bird cry—
the sound made by a seagull on the Hardanger Fjord.*

Seven Songs for Children, Opus 61, are like a breath
of fresh air straight from sea and mountain. This collection contains the lively *Fisherman's Song,* a song such as
Grieg heard many a time on his rambles along the old
wharf and through the fishmarket of Bergen.

An amusing tale was once told by the musician Johan
Bögh. He crossed the market one day with Grieg. "What
a disgusting smell of fish!" exclaimed Bögh.

"You call that disgusting?" shouted Grieg. "Why, it's
simply inspiring!"

"Oh, so *that's* where you get your inspiration?" Bögh
gibed.

But Grieg answered perfectly seriously, "Yes, among
other places."

Another of the Children's Songs is the bewitching
Evening Song for Brownie:

> "Dream of it, old Brownie,
> Nothing to do but eat and rest,
> To trot around the yard at most,
> With the little lad on your back."

In 1894, Grieg composed *Two Norwegian Melodies,*
for string orchestra, Opus 63. The first of these was based
on a folk tune by F. Due, called *In the Folk Tone.* It is
both a folk melody and a nature impression.† The second
was made up of Grieg's own *Cowkeeper's Tune* and
Peasant Dance. In *Cowkeeper's Tune* Grieg has captured

* See Appendix, page 261.
† See Appendix, page 262.

the combined peace and melancholy of the herder's life.*
In *Peasant Dance,* he has evoked the free, unfettered
mood of the folk who dwell aloof on the mountains and
in remote valleys.†

In *Lyrical Pieces,* for piano, Opus 65, Grieg set down
a scene at Troldhaugen. This is the festive *Wedding Day
at Troldhaugen,* dedicated to Nina and presented to her
with old-fashioned gallantry by her husband on one of
their anniversaries. The robust music suggests a peasant
wedding, with bride in tall Hardanger crown and colorful dress walking with the rustic groom at the head of a
procession of villagers. There is a quiet part toward the
middle of the piece, which suggests the wedding ceremony at the church, and then the merrymaking continues.
The singing, sweet quality of the music of the *Poco tranquillo* part‡ makes this one of Grieg's most effective bits
of composition.

Grieg was receiving many more offers to play and conduct abroad than his health would permit his accepting.
Even so, he went on tour too often, complaining all the
while that "a public life is poison."

In December 1896 Grieg gave a concert for the first
time in Vienna. Brahms was living in Vienna and
promptly invited Grieg and their friend Julius Röntgen
to come to his home in the Carlsgasse. The three of them
lunched at Brahms' favorite restaurant, *Der rote Igel.* In
the evening, Brahms went with Grieg to the concert and

* See Appendix, page 262.
† See Appendix, page 262.
‡ See Appendix, page 263.

sat on the platform while his friend from Norway conducted.

The concert was a tremendous success. Grieg bowed himself out to the thunderous cheering and applause of the delighted audience. That evening there was a celebration in Grieg's hotel. The banquet was in Grieg's honor, and the principal speech of the evening was made by Grieg himself. He spoke not a word about his own success in Vienna; his praise was all for his fellow-composer Brahms. For some time past, Brahms had been ill—a little discouraged, too, it may be. The heart-warming words of his Norwegian friend were a balm to his spirit. Tears filled the German composer's eyes. When Grieg had finished speaking, Brahms rose and silently pressed his friend's hand. The two great men of music in that wordless moment saluted the flame of genius which burned so brightly within them both.

There was something of the old fire-eater in him to the end, in spite of his ill health. In 1899, he indignantly refused an offer to appear in the Châtelet Theater in Paris because of the outcome of the Dreyfus affair.

Five years before—in 1894—a young Jewish officer in the French army, Alfred Dreyfus from Alsace-Lorraine, had been accused by the General Staff of the French army of selling military secrets to a foreign power. His military trial was carried out in suspicious secrecy, and he was sentenced to life on the notorious Devil's Island off the coast of South America. To the end, Dreyfus maintained his innocence, and his friends declared that he was the vic-

tim of a conspiracy—that he had been made the scapegoat
to protect a really guilty person in high place.

In 1896 Colonel Picquart, newly appointed head of the
Intelligence Bureau, discovered evidence that the docu-
ment which had been used to convict Dreyfus was a
forgery. When he communicated his findings to his
superior officers, they warned him to say nothing more
about the matter. Picquart then knew for certain that
Dreyfus was innocent. He began to agitate for a review of
the case and was immediately removed from his post and
sent to Africa.

The fat was in the fire, however, and the case became
an affair of world importance. Emile Zola, the famous
French novelist, published his sensational letter exposing
the facts of the case. This was the letter called *"J'accuse"*
(I Accuse).

Not only France but the whole world took sides, until
the contest to free Dreyfus became a struggle of powerful
social and political forces. The monarchists, aristocrats,
and reactionary Church orders sided against Dreyfus; re-
publicans, socialists, and intellectuals of all kinds took his
part, demanding a new trial for a man generally thought
innocent.

In 1899 the new trial was forced by the pressure of
public opinion, but the court of military judges in the
second trial was as hostile as the first had been. The
judges feared the wrath of the people, however; so they
reduced Dreyfus' sentence from life to ten years, with
the five already served to be deducted. The President of

France, afraid to face his people and the world after this
shameful decision, pardoned Dreyfus. But this was not
what Dreyfus and his friends wanted, for "pardon" im-
plied that guilt had existed. They wanted complete exon-
eration for a man who had been convicted on forged
evidence and perjured testimony.

Björnson and Grieg, who had worked in their own
country publicizing the case, getting people to write their
protests to the French authorities, were furious over this
persecution of Dreyfus. That is why Grieg answered
Edouard Colonne, the eminent conductor who invited
him to come to Paris, with this letter:

"Like all other non-Frenchmen, I am shocked at the
injustice in your country and do not feel able to enter into
any relation whatsoever with the French public."

This statement was published in German newspapers.
The rabid enemies of Dreyfus were bitter toward Grieg,
and for some time he received insulting letters and threats
of bodily harm if he came to France. Grieg met that chal-
lenge by going to France, in 1903, when he accepted a
second invitation to play at the Châtelet Theater.

The press of France called for a demonstration against
him. So great was the agitation that he was given police
protection to and from the theater. In the theater he was
met with boos and hisses from hoodlums in the audience.
Not to be turned from his purpose, Grieg signaled the
orchestra to begin. Describing the incident, Grieg wrote
his brother:

"But when I turned toward the orchestra to begin, the
hissing and shouting . . . in chorus in the rhythm of the

Troll King's Daughter got so uncontrollable that I had to put down the baton, step down, and wait quietly to see what would happen. There was a wild fight, but the whole thing was drowned in the most tremendous applause, while meantime the worst disturbers of the peace were thrown out by a *trebled* police force." After that the concert went off "with steadily increasing sympathy from the audience. . . . And afterwards ovations such as—they say here—no French composer has ever had."

Grieg's courage, his winning personality, his brilliant playing and conducting of his own great compositions—all combined to restore him to the favor which he had enjoyed previously in Paris. Of Grieg's popularity among Frenchmen, which almost equaled his popularity among Englishmen, the eminent French composer Gabriel Fauré had once written (in *Le Figaro,* 1893):

"Among the most famous living musicians there is none I know of whose popularity equals, with us, that of Mr. Grieg; none whose works have entered into our inmost musical life in the same degree as have his compositions, which are so full of simple charm, so fine, strange, ever individual. . . ."

Gabriel Fauré, Camille Saint-Saëns, Charles Gounod—the great men of French music whom Grieg admired and to whom he paid homage in frequent critical comment—these men had continued to praise the work of the little Norwegian in the face of popular disapproval of a foreigner who meddled in French politics. Only Claude Debussy had allowed his political bias in the Dreyfus case to color his judgment to the extent that he was guilty of publicly insulting Grieg's art. This ill-mannered outburst was never referred to by Grieg and never dimmed his sincere appreciation of the work of the French impressionist.

After the concert at the Châtelet, the French public joined their country's artists in forgiving Grieg his outspoken criticisms. Once again the artist in Grieg had triumphed for the man.

Grieg had as great a fear that progress would pass him by, that he would be unable to comprehend new ideas, as he had that his creative powers were waning. He once said:

"To be left lying half-forgotten by the wayside while time marches on over my sinful corpse, that seems to me the most wretched fate that can befall a man. And to what countless number does it not happen? Probably to most. But they do not know it and so do not care. It is otherwise with the artist. When he is on the side of reaction he is done."

Certainly Grieg had nothing to fear in this respect, either. Almost to the day of his death he was fighting for fairness and justice, for progress in art and in government. Two of the struggles he interested himself in were brought to a successful conclusion during his lifetime. In 1905, Norway achieved by peaceful means her separation from Sweden. And in 1906, Dreyfus was cleared of all blame, the guilty members of the army were punished, and Dreyfus was restored to his position in the military.

Grieg, fuming and fretting when the creative mood did not come to him, continued to have certain periods of inspiration when he did remarkable work. The songs inspired by the Haugtussa poems—*Eight Songs,* Opus 67 —were the result of one of these spells. *The Mountain Maid, Bilberry Slope,* and *Little Goat's Dance* are charming pictures of Norwegian farm and saeter life.

Grieg's ninth book of *Lyrical Pieces,* Opus 68, contains the fresh and vigorous *Sailors' Shanty.** And he himself was so much pleased with *Evening in the Mountains* from the same opus that he later arranged the piece for oboe and string orchestra. There is the subtle enchantment of the wild upland fells in this music.†

* See Appendix, page 264.
† See Appendix, page 264.

Chapter Twenty

Fear no more the frown o' the great,
Thou are past the tyrant's stroke:
Care no more to clothe and eat;
To thee the reed is as the oak.

CYMBELINE

THE last three years of Grieg's life saw many fine short pieces come into being. His last book of *Lyrical Pieces,* Opus 71, contains several compositions in piquant Norwegian rhythms. In 1902 he began a very important work—*Norwegian Peasants' Dances,* Opus 72, adaptations for piano of the actual dances played by Knut Dale, a fiddler who played in the manner of Möllargutten. One of the dances thus made available and understandable to all the world is *Maiden from Kivletal,** in the *gangar* rhythm. This song has an interesting background of story.

In Selljord in Telemarken there is a valley called Kivletal. Long ago a little church stood in the valley. One

* See Appendix, page 264.

Sunday the congregation was disturbed by loud sounds
from the mountainside—sounds produced by the three
maidens of Kivletal, the last heathen left in the valley.
They were taking turns blowing *slåts* on the Trill-horn.
The church people rushed out to listen with delight to the
enchanting tones. Only the parson was displeased. He
commanded the maidens to stop their playing. When
they would not, he raised his arms to heaven and called
down a curse on their heads. The maidens and their herd
of goats were immediately turned to stone, where they
may be seen (say the villagers of Kivletal) to this very
day on the slopes of the mountain, the maids standing
with their goats around them.

Three magic *slåts* were credited to these maidens. Only
the best fiddlers could learn the music. Only he who
knew all three airs was considered great.

The year before his death, Grieg composed his collection of *Moods,* Opus 73. The best of these compositions
is *Mountaineer's Song.** In this folklike tune he caught
the strange beauty of life lived in the peaceful solitudes
of the high pastures.

Grieg's very last work was a collection of *Four Psalms,*
Opus 74, based on old Norwegian church melodies. With
these magnificent chorales for mixed choir *a capella*
(without accompaniment) Grieg closed his career. His
brave spirit, which acknowledged no defeat in everyday
human affairs, had to accept the bitter demands of an
aging and ailing body.

When his pain-racked body gave him a little peace,
he could be philosophical about his trouble. To Dr. Abra-

* See Appendix, page 265.

ham he wrote: "Just as in true music it is not a question only of crescendo and fortissimo, but also of diminuendo, so life too shows the same shading. We are done now with crescendo and fortissimo. Now we shall play diminuendo. And even a diminuendo *can* be beautiful. Nor is the thought of the coming pianissimo so unsympathetic to me, but for what is ugly in the diminuendo (suffering) I have the greatest respect."

When he had bad days, he could not be so patient. In his diary he wrote, on July 13, 1907: "Ten dreary days which have convinced me that I am going more rapidly downhill than I had thought. . . . If only there were some way of sleeping away into the great sleep when I cannot bear it any longer!"

The last two months of his life Grieg was cheered by visits from his old friend Julius Röntgen and from the young Australian pianist, Percy Grainger. Grieg was carried away by the artistry and personality of Grainger.

"What an artist, what a man!" he wrote in his diary. "What a high idealist, what a child, and, at the same time, what a broad and developed outlook on life. . . . Like a god, he is lifted high over all suffering, all struggle. But one feels they have been there, but are overcome. It is a man, a great and distinguished man who plays. May life go well for him!"

Grieg's illness grew rapidly worse; yet he was actually planning a concert tour just before his death in Bergen hospital. Nina went to the hospital with him and stayed with him to the very last. His last words to Nina were, "Well, if it must be so." Then like a tired child he closed his eyes.

There was a state funeral. The bells of Bergen tolled sorrowfully for the illustrious son of the great Westland of Norway. Nina and her sister, and two of Grieg's sisters, walked beside the hearse.

As the composer had wished, the *Funeral March for Nordraak* was played as the procession made its way from church to street. The mournful chords of the march followed the little Viking to his last resting place.

Grieg's ashes were placed in a natural grotto in the face of a wall of rock below Troldhaugen, looking west toward the fjord. Frants Beyer wrote to Nina to tell her that he and Schack Bull had carried out Grieg's own wish in placing the urn in the grotto shielded by a thicket of birch and spruce, bird cherry and rowan:

"Dear Nina!

"And so Edvard's ashes have now come to their last resting place. I deeply hope you will feel satisfied with the grotto and the whole thing. It was a quiet, soft spring day when in the afternoon Schack and I brought the urn . . . in a closed carriage to Troldhaugen. I set the urn in the grotto and then the stone was put in place. A blackbird sang in the spruces above. Just at that moment the sun went down behind the clouds edged with gold and cast its last rays over the water upon Edvard's name.

"Dear Nina, it will be so dear and precious to you to have the grotto so near, and there is a wonderful peace and beauty over the spot Edvard himself has chosen.

"May his ashes rest in peace!"

APPENDICES

Edvard Grieg's Works

NOTE: *Compositions marked with an asterisk have been recorded. However, the difficulties of importing records from Europe have recently so affected the stocks of American record dealers that no assurance can be offered that any given recording can now be bought. Also, it will be advisable, in asking for records, to specify opus numbers, since record labels sometimes carry titles differing from the originals.*

Opus No.	Name of Composition
1	Four Pieces for piano
2	Four Songs for contralto:

    1. The Mill Girl
    2. Dark dreams possess me
    3. I am encompassed by gray clouds
    4. What shall I say?

| 3 | Six Poetic Tone Pictures for piano |
| 4 | Six Songs: |

    1. The Orphan
    2. Morning Dew
    3. There was an old king
    4. Where did they go?
    5. Departure
    6. Hunter's Song

| 5 | Four Songs: |

    1. Canst gather the speech of the ocean's swell?
    2. The Poet's Heart
    *3. I love thee
    4. My mind is like a mountain steep

| 6 | Humoresques for piano |

Opus No.	Name of Composition
7	Sonata in E minor for piano
8	Sonata for Violin and Piano, No. 1, F major
9	Four Songs:

    1. The Harp
    2. Cradle Song
    3. At Sunset
    4. Outward Bound

10   Four Songs:
    1. Thanksgiving
    2. Forest Songs
    3. The flowers speak
    4. Song on the Mountains

11   In the Autumn: Concert Overture (arranged also for piano, four hands)

12   Lyrical Pieces for piano, Book I:
    *1. Arietta
    2. Waltz
    3. Watchman's Song
    *4. Dance of the Elves
    *5. Folk Song
    *6. Norwegian
    7. Album Leaf
    8. Song of the Fatherland

13   *Sonata for Violin and Piano, No. 1, G major

14   Two Symphonic Pieces for piano duet

15   Four Songs:
    1. Margaret's Cradle Song
    2. Love
    3. Folksong from Langeland
    4. Mother Sorrow

16   *Piano Concerto, in A minor (also arranged for two pianos)

Opus No.	Name of Composition
17	Northern Dances (based on the Lindeman collection "Old and New Mountain Melodies"):

1. Dance
2. The Youngster
3. Dance
4. Niels Tallefjoren
5. Jólster's Dance
6. Betrothal Song
7. Halling
8. Religious Song
9. Song
10. Heroic Song
11. Solfager
12. Traveler's Song
13. Funeral Song
14. The Last Saturday Night
15. I know a young girl
16. Comic Dance
17. Hölje Dale
18. Halling
19. Sacygga
20. Dance of the Cows
21. Country Song
22. Song
23. Wedding of the Crow

18	Eight Songs:

1. Woodland Wandering
2. So white is she
3. A Poet's Last Song
4. Autumn Storm
5. Poesy

Opus No.	Name of Composition
18	6. The Rosebud
Contd.	7. The Hut
	8. The Young Birch
19	Sketches of Norwegian Life for piano:
	1. Mountain Dance
	*2. The bridal procession passes by
	3. From the Carnival
20	At the Cloister Gate, for soprano and alto solo, women's chorus, and orchestra
21	Four Songs:
	*1. First Meeting
	*2. Good Morning
	3. My song to the Spring I proffer
	4. Your advice is good
22	*Two Songs from *Sigurd Jorsalfar,* for solo, men's chorus, and orchestra:
	*1. The Norse People
	*2. King's Song
23	Songs from *Peer Gynt:*
	1. Solvejg's Song (arranged also for concert performance, with orchestra)
	2. Solvejg's Slumber Song (arranged also for concert performance, with orchestra)
	3. Peer Gynt's Serenade
24	*Ballade in G minor for piano
25	Five Songs:
	1. Minstrel's Song
	*2. A Swan (arranged also for concert performance, with orchestra)
	3. Departed
	*4. With a Waterlily
	5. Bird Song

Opus No.	Name of Composition
26	Four Songs:

        1. Hope

        2. A lovely summer evening 'twas

        3. Wood Wandering

     *4. The First Primrose

27   *String Quartet, in G minor

28   Four Album Leaves, for piano (No. 3*)

29   Improvisation on Two Norwegian Folk Songs, for piano

30   Album of Part Songs, for men's voices:

        1. So late I went to sleep

        2. Nursery Song ("Trumma rumma rum bumm")

        3. Pretty Torö

        4. Halling

        5. This is surely the biggest fool!

        6. If I do go out of an evening

        7. Young Ole

        8. Halling

        9. Loveliest among women

    *10. The Great White Host

     11. Good-for-Nothing

     12. There Goes Knut

31   *Landsighting, for baritone solo and men's chorus

32   Taken into the Mountains, baritone solo, string orchestra, two horns

33   Twelve Songs:

        1. The Youth

     *2. Springtide (arranged also for concert performance, with orchestra)

     *3. Wounded

      4. The Berry

Opus No.	Name of Composition
33 Contd.	5. At the Brookside
	6. A Vision
	*7. The Old Mother
	8. The First Thing
	9. On the Journey Home
	10. Friendship
	11. Faith
	12. My Goal
34	Two Elegiac Melodies, for string orchestra
	*1. Heart Wounds
	*2. The Last Spring
35	*Four Norwegian Dances, for four hands:
	*1. (Built on the Sinclair march from Vågå)
	2. Halling from Åmot
	*3. Halling
	*4. Dance
36	*Sonata for Violoncello and Piano in A minor
37	Two Waltz-Caprices, for piano, four hands
38	Lyrical Pieces, for piano, Book II:
	1. Berceuse
	2. Folk Song
	3. Melody
	4. Norwegian Dance (Halling)
	5. Springdans
	6. Elegy
	7. Waltz
	8. Canon
39	Five Songs:
	*1. From Monte Pincio (also arranged for concert performance, with orchestra)
	2. Hidden Love
	3. On the High Hillsides

Opus No.   *Name of Composition*

4. 'Neath the Roses

5. At the Bier of a Young Woman

6. When to that song I listen

40   From Holberg's Time, for string orchestra (originally written as a piano solo):

1. Prelude

2. Sarabande

3. Gavotte

4. Air

5. Rigaudon

41   Six Songs, transcribed for piano:

1. Cradle Song

2. Little Haakon

3. I love thee

4. When once she lay

5. The Princess

6. To Spring

42   Bergliot, poem for declamation with orchestra

43   Lyrical Pieces, for piano, Book III:

*1. Butterfly

2. Lonely Wanderer

3. In My Native Country

4. Little Bird

*5. Erotik

*6. To Spring

44   Four Songs from Fjeld and Fjord:

Prologue

1. Joan

2. Ragna

3. Ragnhild

4. Ingeborg

Epilogue

Opus No.	Name of Composition
45	*Sonata for Violin and Piano, No. 3, A minor
46	*Peer Gynt Suite, No. 1, for orchestra:

    1. Morning Mood
    2. Åse's Death
    3. Anitra's Dance
    4. In the Hall of the Mountain King

47   Lyrical Pieces, for piano, Book IV:

    1. Valse-Impromptu
    2. Album Leaf
    3. Melody
    4. Halling
    5. Melancholy
    6. Springdans
    7. Elegie

48   Six Songs:

    1. Greeting
    2. Ere long, O heart of mine
    *3. The Way of the World
    4. The Silent Nightingale
    5. In Time of Roses
    *6. A Dream

49   Six Songs:

    1. Christmas Snow
    2. Spring Rain
    3. Now is the evening bright and warm
    4. Rock, O waves
    5. Did you see the lad pass by?
    6. Salute to the Ladies

50   Olaf Trygvason, for solo voices, chorus, and orchestra

51   Old Norwegian Romance with Variations, for two pianos (arranged also for full orchestra)

Opus No.   *Name of Composition*

52   Six Songs, transcribed for piano:
            1. Mother Sorrow
            2. First Meeting
            3. The Poet's Heart
            4. Solvejg's Song
            5. Love
            6. The Old Mother

53   Two Songs, transcribed for string orchestra:
            1. Norsk (Norwegian)
            2. First Meeting

54   Lyrical Pieces, for piano, Book V:
            *1. Shepherd Boy
            *2. Gangar
            *3. March of the Dwarfs
            *4. Notturno
            5. Scherzo
            6. Bell Ringing

55   *Peer Gynt Suite, No. II:
            1. Abduction of the Bride and Ingrid's
                Lament
            2. Arab Dance
            3. Peer Gynt's Homecoming
            4. Solvejg's Song

56   *Sigurd Jorsalfar: Three pieces for orchestra:
            1. Overture: In the King's Hall
            2. Intermezzo: Borghild's Dream
            3. Triumphal March

57   Lyrical Pieces, for piano, Book VI:
            1. Vanished Days
            2. Gade
            3. Illusion

Opus No.	*Name of Composition*
57	4. The Secret
Contd.	5. She dances
	6. Longing for Home
	7. Minuet
58	Five Songs:
	1. Homecoming
	2. From the Fatherland
	3. Henrik Wergeland (arranged also for concert performance, with orchestra)
	4. The Herd-Girl
	5. The Wanderer
59	Six Songs:
	1. Autumn Mood
	2. The Fir Tree
	3. You are the youth Lenz
	4. Why do your eyes sparkle?
	5. Departure
	6. Now you are at rest
60	Five Songs:
	1. Pretty Marg'ret
	2. The Mother Sings
	*3. In the Boat
	4. A bird flew screaming
	*5. On St. John's Eve
61	Seven Songs for Children:
	*1. Ah, green and glittering tree
	2. The Norwegian Mountains
	*3. Hymn to the Fatherland
	4. The Ocean
	5. Call
	6. Fisherman's Song
	7. Evening Song for Brownie

Opus No.	Name of Composition

62   Lyrical Pieces, for piano, Book VII:

1. Sylfide
2. Thanks
3. French Serenade
4. The Brook
5. Dream Vision
6. Homeward Bound

63   Two Norwegian Melodies, for string orchestra:

1. Im Volkston
2. Cowkeeper's Tune and Peasant Dance

64   *Symphonic Dances, for piano, four hands (also arranged for large orchestra)

65   Lyrical Pieces, for piano, Book VIII:

1. From Youthful Days
2. Peasant's Song
3. Melancholy
4. Salon
5. In Ballad Style
*6. Wedding Day at Troldhaugen

66   Popular Norwegian Melodies, for piano (19 folk tunes):

1. Love-Call
2. It is the greatest foolishness
3. A king reigned
4. The Legend of Siri Dale
5. It was in my youth
6. Love-Call and Child's Song
7. Lullaby
8. Love-Call
9. Little was the boy
10. Tomorrow shall you wedded be
11. There were two maidens
12. Ranveïg

Opus No.	*Name of Composition*
66	13. A Little Gray Man
Contd.	14. In Ola Valley
	15. Lullaby
	16. Little Astrid
	17. Lullaby
	18. Thoughtfully I wander
	19. Gjendine's Cradle Song
67	*Haugtussa—Eight Songs:
	1. Song
	2. The Mountain Maid
	3. Bilberry Slope
	4. The Tryst
	5. Love
	6. Little Goat's Dance
	7. An Evil Day
	8. By the Gjaetle-Brook
68	Lyrical Pieces, for piano, Book IX:
	1. Sailors' Shanty
	2. Grandmother's Minuet
	3. At thy feet
	4. Valse Mélancolique
	5. Lullaby
	6. Evening on the Mountain (arranged also for oboe and string orchestra)
69	Five Songs:
	1. A boat on the waves is rocking
	2. To My Boy
	3. At Mother's Grave
	4. Snail, Snail!
	5. Dreams
70	Five Songs:
	*1. Eros
	2. I live a life of longing

Opus No.   *Name of Composition*

        3. Light Night

        4. Take Care!

        5. Poet's Song

71   Lyrical Pieces, for piano, Book X:

        1. Once upon a time

        2. Summer's Eve

        3. Kobold

        4. Peace of the Woods

        5. Halling

        6. Gone

        7. Echo

72   Norwegian Peasant Dances:

        1. Giböen's Wedding March

      *2. Jon Vestafaes' Springdans

        3. Wedding March from Telemark

        4. Dance of the Gnomes

        5. Springdans

        6. Gangar after Möllarguten

        7. Rotnam's Hill

        8. Brautmarsch

        9. Nils Rekve's Halling

      10. Knut Lurasen's Halling I

      11. Knut Lurasen's Halling II

      12. Springdans

      13. Springdans

      14. Gangar

      15. Gangar

      16. Maiden from Kivletal (Gangar)

      17. Springdans from Selljord

73   Moods, for piano:

        1. Resignation

      *2. Scherzo impromptu

        3. A Nocturnal Ride

Opus No.	Name of Composition
73 Contd.	4. Folktone
	5. Etude (Homage to Chopin)
	6. Student's Serenade
	7. Mountaineer's Song
74	Four Psalms, for mixed choir a capella:

      *1. God's Son hath set me free

      2. Jesus Christ is risen

      3. How fair is Thy face

      4. In Heaven

Without opus number:

Funeral March for Nordraak

Quartet in F major (completed by Röntgen)

The Odalisque

Ave Maris Stella

*The Princess (piano transcription of this song—Opus 41, No. 5)

PIANO PIECE

Opus 1, No. 1

POETIC TONE PICTURES, III

Opus 3, No. 3

SONG—THERE WAS A KING

Opus 4, No. 3

243

SONG—I LOVE THEE

Opus 5, No. 3

MENUETTO FROM HUMORESQUES

Opus 6, No. 2

ANDANTE FROM PIANO SONATA

Opus 7

AUTUMN STORM

Opus 18, No. 4

OUTWARD BOUND

Opus 9

AUTUMN

Opus II

WATCHMAN'S SONG
Opus 12, No. 3

(composed after witnessing a performance of Shakespeare's "Macbeth")

SONG OF THE FATHERLAND
Opus 12, No. 8

MARGARET'S CRADLE SONG
Opus 15, No. 1

PIANO CONCERTO IN A MINOR   Opus 16

THE BRIDAL PROCESSION PASSES   Opus 19, No. 2

SONG—THE PRINCESS

Opus 21, No. 4

BALLADE IN G MINOR

Opus 24

ABDUCTION OF THE BRIDE

Opus 55, No. 1

INGRID'S LAMENT

Opus 55, No. I

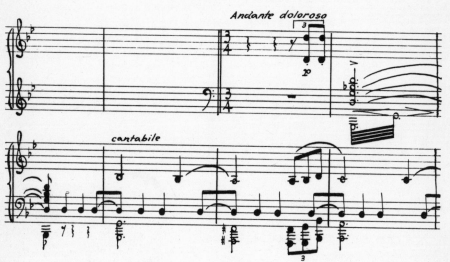

IN THE HALL OF THE MOUNTAIN KING

Opus 46, No. 4

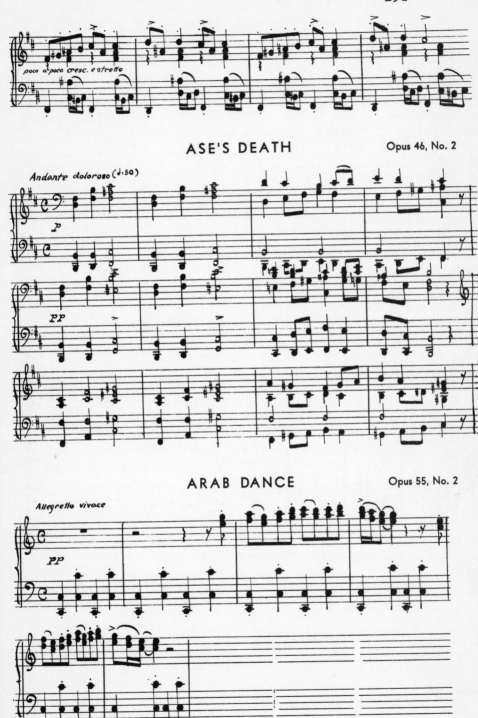

ASE'S DEATH

Opus 46, No. 2

ARAB DANCE

Opus 55, No. 2

ANITRA'S DANCE

Opus 46, No. 3

Tempo di Mazurka

SOLVEJG'S SONG

Opus 23, No. 1

MORNING MOOD

Opus 46, No. 1

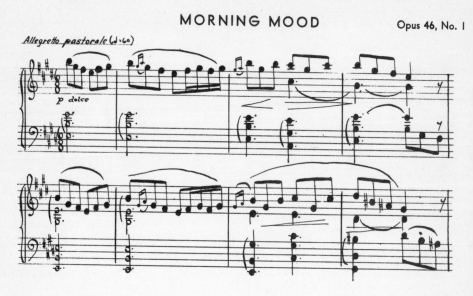

PEER GYNT'S HOMECOMING

Opus 55, No. 3

STRING QUARTET IN G MINOR

Opus 27

DANCE CAPRICE

Opus 28, No. 3

SPRINGTIDE

Opus 33, No. 2

ON THE JOURNEY HOME

Opus 33, No. 9

THE OLD MOTHER

Opus 33, No. 7

NORWEGIAN DANCE
HALLING FROM AMOT

Opus 35, No. 2

SONATA FOR 'CELLO AND PIANO IN A MINOR

Opus 36

BERCEUSE
Opus 38, No. I

Allegretto tranquillo (♩=92)

rit.

FROM HOLBERG'S TIME
Opus 40

Andante religioso (♩=54)
cantabile

LITTLE BIRD

Opus 43, No. 4

TO SPRING

Opus 48, No. 6

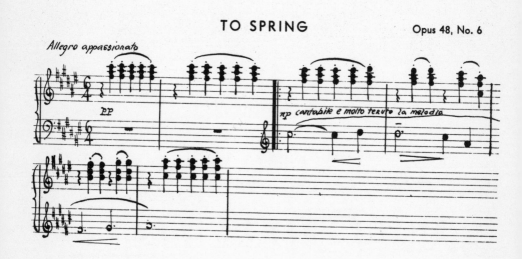

MARCH OF THE DWARFS

Opus 54, No. 3

BELL RINGING

Opus 54, No. 6

A BIRD FLEW SCREAMING

Opus 60, No. 4

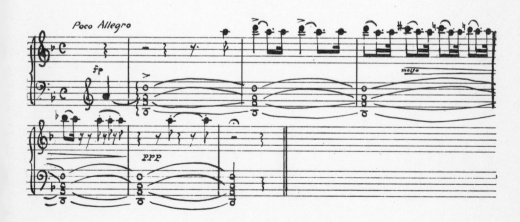

262

IN THE FOLK TONE

Opus 63, No. 1

COWKEEPER'S TUNE

Opus 63, No. 2

PEASANT DANCE

Opus 63, No. 2

WEDDING DAY AT TROLDHAUGEN Opus 65, No. 6

SAILORS' SHANTY

Opus 68, No. 1

EVENING IN THE MOUNTAINS

Opus 68, No. 4

MAIDEN FROM KIVLETAL

Opus 72, No. 16

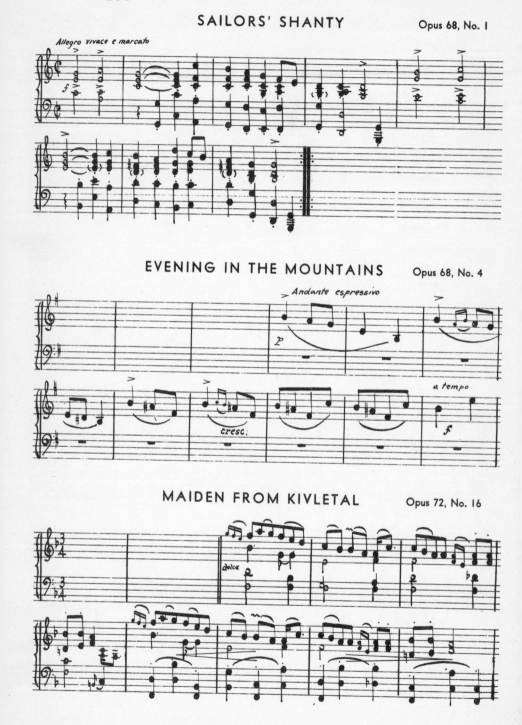

MOUNTAINEER'S SONG

Opus 73, No. 7

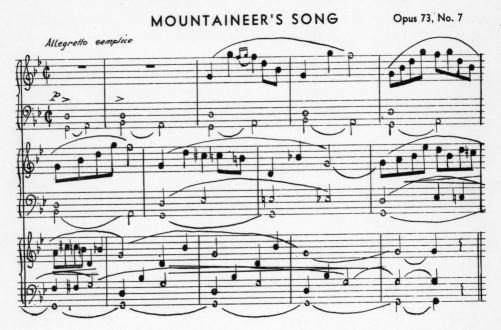

FUNERAL MARCH FOR NORDRAAK

Books and Magazines

USED IN THE PREPARATION OF THIS BOOK

BOOKS

David Monrad-Johansen: *Edvard Grieg*. Translated from the Norwegian by Madge Robertson. Princeton University Press and the American-Scandinavian Foundation, N. Y., 1938.

Daniel Gregory Mason: *From Grieg to Brahms*. The Macmillan Company, N. Y., 1936.

Ernest Closson: *Edvard Grieg et la musique scandinave*. Librairie Fischbacher, Paris, 1892.

Lawrence Gilman: *Nature in Music:* Grieg. John Lane Company, N. Y., 1914.

Paul de Stoecklin: *Grieg*. Librairie Félix Alcan, Paris, 1926.

Henry Theophilus Finck: *Grieg and His Music*. John Lane Company, N. Y., 1909.

M. Gillington: *Days With Great Composers:* "A Day With Edvard Grieg." Hodder & Stoughton, London.

Vocations, Volume IX, "Music and Public Entertainment," edited by Horatio Parker, contains Grieg's "My First Success." Hall & Locke Company, Boston, 1911.

Grieg's Preface to his Opus 72, "Slatter." Peters, Leipzig.

Arthur Elson: *The Book of Musical Knowledge,* Chapter XXV: "Grieg and the Northern Countries." Houghton Mifflin Company, Boston, 1927.

H. M. Brower: *Story Lives of Master Musicians*. Stokes, N. Y., 1922.

Frederic Lawrence: *Musicians of Sorrow and Romance*. C. H. Kelly, London, 1913.

Charles D. Isaacson: *Face to Face With Great Musicians.*
D. Appleton & Company, N. Y., 1921.

Eva v. B. Hansl and Helen L. Kaufmann: *Minute Sketches of Great Composers.* Grosset & Dunlap, N. Y., 1932.

George P. Upton: *Standard Musical Biographies.* A. C. McClurg & Co., Chicago, 1910.

W. Frances Gates: *Anecdotes of Great Musicians.* Theodore Presser Co., Philadelphia, 1895.

The International Library of Music, Volume I: "Critical and Biographical Sketches of the Epoch Makers of Music." The University Society, N. Y., 1925.

Ole Bull: A Memoir, by Sara C. Bull. Houghton Mifflin Company, Boston, 1883.

Rosa Newmarch: *Tschaikovsky, His Life and Works:* "Diary of My Tour in 1888." Dodd, Mead & Company, N. Y.

Percy A. Scholes: *The Oxford Companion to Music.* Oxford University Press, London, 1938.

The American History and Encyclopedia of Music, edited by W. L. Hubbard: "History of Foreign Music—Scandinavia, Norway." Irving Squire, N. Y., 1908.

Baker's Biographical Dictionary of Musicians, Third Edition. G. Schirmer, N. Y., 1919.

Grove's Dictionary of Music and Musicians: "Grieg." The Macmillan Company, N. Y., 1911.

The International Cyclopedia of Music and Musicians, edited by Oscar Thompson: "Grieg." Dodd, Mead & Company, N. Y., 1939.

Jennie Hall: *Viking Tales.* Rand, 1902.

William Patten: "Stories from the Northern Sagas" in *Junior Classics,* Vol. 2.

A. and E. Keary: *The Heroes of Asgard.* The Macmillan Company, N. Y., 1924.

John Arnett MacCulloch: *The Mythology of All Races,* Volume II, Eddic. Archaeological Institute of America and Marshall Jones Company, Boston, 1930.

Paul Du Chaillu: *The Viking Age.* Charles Scribner's Sons, N. Y., 1889.

Hamilton Wright Mabie: *Norse Stories Retold from the Eddas.* Dodd, Mead & Company, N. Y., 1901.

Samuel J. Beckett: *A Wayfarer in Norway.* Robert M. McBride, N. Y., 1936.

Clara E. Laughlin: *Where It All Comes True in Scandinavia.* Houghton Mifflin Co., Boston, 1929.

Sydney A. Clark: *Norway on $50.* Robert M. McBride, N. Y., 1936.

Agnes Rothery: *Norway, Changing and Changeless.* Viking Press, N. Y., 1939.

Dorothy Spicer: *The Book of Festivals.* Womans Press, N. Y., 1937.

CHILDREN'S READING

Franciska Schwimmer: *Great Musicians as Children.* Doubleday, Doran, Garden City, N. Y., 1929.

Mary Newlin Roberts: *Young Masters of Music.* Thomas Y. Crowell Company, N. Y., 1931.

Alethea Cox: *Imaginary Biographical Letters.* Theodore Presser, Philadelphia, 1911.

Marion Bauer: *How Music Grew:* "Grieg"—p. 449. G. P. Putnam's Sons, N. Y., 1928.

Satella S. Waterstone: *Short Stories of Musical Melodies:* Grieg's *Arietta, Watchman's Song,* and *Cradle Song.* P. F. Volland & Company, N. Y., 1915.

Gladys Burch and John Wolcott: *A Child's Book of Famous Composers.* Barnes, N. Y., 1939.

K. D. Cather: "Musician of the Fjords" in *St. Nicholas,* February 1927.

Magazine Articles

A. Trondsen: "Home of Edvard Grieg" in *Mentor*, February 1929.

Percy Grainger: "Glimpses of Genius" in *Etude*, October 1921.

——, "Grieg's Norwegian Bridal Procession" in *Etude*, November 1920.

H. Wetherby: "Great Masters As Students of Music" in *Etude*, March 1928.

D. G. Mason: "Grieg's Style" in *The Musician*, January 1928.

M. M. Schmitz: "Little Life Stories of the Great Masters" in *Etude*, February 1927.

M. Anderton: "How to Study *Butterfly*" in *The Musician*, June 1931.

N. R. Graves: "Grieg's Picturesque Environment Reflected in His Music" in *Etude*, October 1933.

M. A. d'A. Chandler: "Memory Pictures of Famous Musicians" in *Etude*, August 1936.

"My First Success." Tr. by S. H. Lovewell, in *Etude*, October and November 1937.

D. M. Johansen: "Musical Viking" in *Etude*, October 1939.

GENERAL INDEX

INDEX OF GRIEG'S WORKS